# EASTBOURNE'S STORY

## John Surtees

MELIORA SEQUIMUR

S.B. Publications

By the same author
*The House Physician's Handbook*
*Barracks, Workhouse and Hospital, St Mary's Eastbourne*
*The Princess Alice and other Eastbourne hospitals*
*St Wilfrid's the Eastbourne and District Hospice*
*Chaseley, a Home from Home*
*Beachy Head*
*The Strange Case of Dr Bodkin Adams*
*Eastbourne a History*

First published in 2005 by
SB Publications
Tel: 01323 893498

ISBN 1 85770  298 0

*Front cover: Aerial view of Eastbourne seafront 2002 (by Channel Photography)*
*Back cover: Eastbourne Pier, morning light, and the Sovereign Harbour 2003*
*(both by Nick Taylor)*

Typeset by EH Graphics. Tel: 01273 515527
Printed by Ethos Productions Ltd.

# Contents

**Acknowledgements**

My special thanks go to my wife, Sheila, for her help and encouragement. Acknowledgements to Brian Allchorn, Stanley Apps, Steve Benz, Wilf Bignell, Judith Brent, Stephen Brewer, Ann & Alan Caffyn, John Cant, Muriel Childs, Mavis Clack, John V Claremont, Gordon Clark, Michael Clark, Betty & Arthur Cobb, Terry Connolly, J & L Davies-Gilbert, Peter L Drewett, Dorothy Ecroyd, Bob Elliston, John Farrant, Ian H Ford, Lawrence Ford, Paul E Fulford, John Gowland, Alastair Graham, Clive Griggs, Stella Hardwick, Paul Harris, Ken Harrison, Ted Hide, Vera Hodsoll, Maureen Honey, Graham Household, Chris Howden, Elizabeth Howe, Frances Jardine, Lionel Jones, Chris Jordan, Derek Keay, WH Kefford, Harold & Sylvia Kennedy, Lorna Kenward, Norman Kinnish, Percy G Langdon, Jane Leete, Marie Lewis, Peter Longstaff-Tyrrell, Lou McMahon, Pauline Markquick, Rosemary & John Milton, Frances Muncey, Michael Ockenden, SC Nash, Miriam C Nixey, Betty & Peter Palmer, Michael & Tim Partridge, Jack Putland, Nigel Quiney, John Redfern, Brian Robinson, Mary & Tom Searle, Harold D Spears, John & Irene Stevens, Pat & Lawrence Stevens, D Swift, Gillian Tarrant, Nick Taylor, Joan & Ken Thurman, Doreen Toghill, Betty Turner, Ronald Turner, Dr Kenneth Vickery, WJ Vine, Jack Warne, Edgar Williams, Lindsay Woods, Esther Worsfold.

Beckett Publications, British Library, British Museum, Caffyn's plc publicity department, University Library Cambridge, Channel Photography, Eastbourne Local History Society, Eastbourne Town Council minutes, Eastbourne Central Library, Eastbourne Natural History and Archaeological Society, East Sussex Public Record Office, Hastings Museum, Walter Llewellyn & Sons Ltd ROK, Museum of History of Science Oxford University, National Portrait Gallery, Science & Society Picture Library, Towner Art Gallery and History Museum, National Archive, Kew.

Whilst every effort has been made to contact relevant individuals and organisations, it is regretted that at the time of going to press it has not been possible to publish all the names. Those concerned are asked to accept the author's apologies.

It took over 15 million years for the chalk of Beachy Head to be formed from the remains of small sea creatures. This was about 100 million years ago, when dinosaurs roamed the earth. The chalk was later lifted up clear of the sea. Evidence has been found that a mere million years ago elephants roamed round the site of the railway station, and hippopotamus and rhinoceros teeth have been found around the pedestrian precinct. Man came only a few 100 000 years ago, and then sporadically.

# 1. A 'New Town' that goes back a long way

Yes, you could say that it was only after sea bathing came in and the Royal holiday visit of 1780 that Eastbourne became a town. Certainly after the railway brought the holidaymakers, the town rapidly developed from tiny, straggling farming villages and a few fishermen into the 'Empress of Watering Places'.

Just as easily, however, you could argue that the story goes back thousands of years. Some 10 000 years ago, with the Ice Age at an end, the many lakes left by the melting ice broke through to create the Channel. As today the coastline was changing, chalk falls eroding Beachy Head, and an inlet to the east was building up a shingle bank, the Crumbles, now dug out for the Sovereign Harbour.

Early man tended to live on top of the Downs to give warning of attack and to avoid the forbidding, impenetrable Wealden forest. Beachy Head has evidence of Stone Age, Bronze Age and later Iron Age man, with Belle Tout boasting the only site in south-east England for the Beaker People of 4000 years ago.

Four bracelets were found on Beachy Head, at Heathy Brow, an Iron Age settlement with mixed farming, mainly sheep.

Funerary pot of the Bronze Age (about 4000 to 2700 years ago locally) found on Bullock Down, Beachy Head, where a number have been discovered.

Iron Age pot found buried in Green Street. We know it was made here because it had gone wrong in the firing, and the potter buried it as he didn't want his mistake to be seen.

The Romans came 2000 years ago, followed by Saxons, Vikings and Danes and, after the Battle of Hastings, the Normans. So there was quite a lot of life and death, although, apart from the Romans, bathing was not on the menu.

The 700 years of the Iron Age lasted until the **Romans** came in 43AD to stay for 400 years. They were welcomed by the locals, whose king, Cogidubnus, had traded with the invaders. The Romans ran a corn/sheep system, with more corn acreage on the Downs than ever, providing food for the local populace, the Romans, and for export. A large villa appeared near the present pier, with three farmsteads on Beachy Head. So there was opulence here before the Royals.

The Roman villa was unearthed in 1712, and as was the fashion, the mosaics were exposed and broken up for building rubble. Discoveries in 1841, and 1851-3 at Grand Parade, were also built over, so no structures are to be seen, but Roman coins and pottery have been found all over the town.

The Romans introduced the locals to all the Roman delights such as decent roads and vertical walls, and from central heating and nails to ointments and locks, as well as law and security. The Saxon Shore fort of Andritum at Pevensey, that the Romans completed in 335, is the only obvious remnant of those times. The site jutted into a sea inlet which was dotted with islets, or 'Eyes', a term perpetuated in Hydneye and Anten's Eye (St Anthony's Hill) among others.

Roman tessera, or floor tiles, found at Eastbourne, now in the Towner Museum.

Saxon fish brooch from a female grave at Ocklynge.

After the Romans left c.400 the **Saxons** from Germany, who had been raiding the coast for years, landed near Chichester in 477. It was said that at Pevensey they slaughtered the last Celtic defenders to a man. Celtic names or ways were obliterated so that by 600 Sussex was a South Saxon kingdom.

Although most Britons had been Christian in Roman times, many had lapsed or reverted to paganism. Sussex was about the last English county to be converted, around 680 by St Wilfrid, who having found the inhabitants in the throes of a famine and throwing themselves off the cliffs, taught them how to fish.

You are at a Saxon crossroads, if you stand by the High Street and Borough Lane. From the number of graves in Ocklynge the Saxons stayed for hundreds of years. When the College of Technology was demolished in 1997 another Saxon cemetery was discovered, with some Christian and some pagan burials.

The first mention of 'Bourne' is in 963. Fresh water decided where Eastbourne should be, as well as providing its name. Rainwater soaks through the porous chalk Downs until it comes to an impervious layer of gault clay where springs run out to the surface. A spring does just that at Motcombe pond from where the Bourne Stream issues on the way to the sea.

The next wave of boat-invaders were the **Vikings**, or **Danes**, in 790, but the efforts of King Alfred the Great gave the country a century of peace. Eastbourne even became part of his Royal estate, so perhaps Alfred burnt his cakes here.

The Danes returned with King Canute ruling over much of southern England. In

1054, Edward the Confessor's time, there is a record of a wooden church in Eastbourne, possibly on Willingdon hill, but as so often no trace remains.

On 28 September 1066 William of Normandy tripped ashore at Norman's Bay, just by Pevensey, or so some believe. When, a couple of weeks later, he defeated the Saxon King Harold at **Hastings** he become William the Conqueror. He was energetic and able and before long all England was in the hands of his relatives and supporters. Eastbourne was given to the Count of Mortain, a half-brother, who like all the Normans made his presence felt by starting to build an imposing castle from which to look down on his subjects, in his case within the Roman fort at Pevensey.

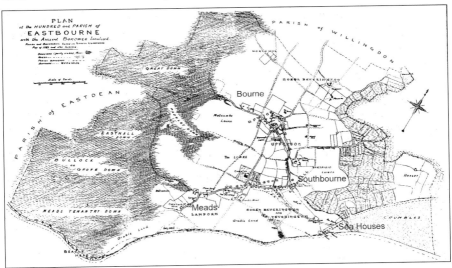

The shaded areas are Downland to the left and the summer meadows to the right. As shown on this map of 1783, there were four separate hamlets before 1800. The largest was **Bourne** or Old Town, tucked away from the winds and storms; **Sea Houses** - fishermen's cottages on the coast near today's Queens Hotel; **Southbourne** the area of Grove Road and South Street; and **Meads** to the west, yet to become the posh part of the town, was nothing more than a couple of farms.

At least Eastbourne got a mention in William's Domesday Book, when Bourne had a church, '1 mill at 5/-', saltpans, and some 350 people.

Eventually, in 1308, Edward II gave the Manor of Bourne to Bartholomew de Badlesmere. He never lived at Eastbourne, but he had Eastbourne's Parish Church extended, and was granted charters for a market and fair. Afterwards he rebelled against the king, was hanged and his estates forfeited.

The estates were restored to his family in 1330, and they fell to William, Lord de Roos, whose family held Bourne in an almost continuous line until 1555.

Badlesmere's fair developed into a sheep fair, with the sheep penned on Summerdown. The Rector of Eastbourne had already been granted a charter in 1232 to hold a three-day fair at Michaelmas, and this continued for 670 years into the early 1900s. In the absence of shops it was almost the only opportunity to buy goods, and a fine excuse for merchants and farmers to frequent the *Lamb Inn.*

Around about Eastbourne is ideal for mixed farming; sheep do not need as much water as cattle and prefer less lush grass, so they do well on the Downland turf, while the lower slopes of the Downs have rich land suitable for arable or dairy farming. Cattle would be driven to the marshy meadows at Pevensey for summer fattening – hence Pashley and Willingdon Droves.

St Mary's Church c.1875. It dates from 1160. Of Caen stone, chequered flints and greensand; extended in the 1300s and restored in Victorian times. The chancel inclines southward, and is below the nave level. Masons' marks are seen in the chancel and on arches, and there are tablet brasses to John King 1445 and James Graves 1647. The central east window is fine Early Decorated, as are the wooden screens. The north aisle windows, the font and tower are Perpendicular, while the south aisle has c.1620 hood mouldings.

The Black Death, which severely affected Sussex, caused an extreme shortage of labour. These changes threatened the medieval system of serfs working strips of land under the Lord of the Manor, and as sheep farming increased and as English wool became famed on the continent, Eastbourne became richer.

With over 4000 sheep on the nearby Downs there were more sheep than people, and agriculture continued as the prime occupation until the 1800s.

The local farmers were doing so well that when in 1555 the Earl of Rutland, a consort of the de Roos family, divided the Manor of Eastbourne into 22 parts for sale, three farmers bought the lot. They were the Burtons of *Bourne Place,* later *Compton Place,* who took 280 acres; the Gildredges who had their 'sub-manor house' in The Goffs; and the Selwyns of *Friston Place.*

Eastbourne probably had a beacon near Beachy Head to warn of the Armada, but otherwise it wasn't well prepared for the Spanish fleet. The 1587 Survey found only ancient guns with 'no powder and shot', and it does appear that the town underwent a recession around 1600, with 1616 an especially bad plague year.

At least the Civil War passed Eastbourne by, although the local gentry were divided in their allegiances. At *Bourne Place* when Parliamentary troops came to make an inspection they were served a dish of wheatear pie, considered a special delicacy, giving the hosts time to destroy any incriminating Royalist documents.

Wheatears are migrating birds that the local shepherds trapped in great numbers on the Downs to augment their larder and purse. In 1799 a local shepherd was said to have trapped 1200 in one day.

In 1664 *Bourne Place* was sold to the Wilsons, relatives of the Burtons; the Gildredge estate became Gilbert by marriage in 1668, while the Ratton part of the Selwyn lands went to the Parker family, again as part of a marriage dowry.

*Compton Place* c.1870. Was *Bourne Place* until Spencer Compton bought it in 1724. He already owned Sussex properties from his step-mother Lady Isabel Sackville. *Compton Place* has been owned by the Cavendish family since 1782, but leased out to a language school since the 1950s.

Already a middle class was appearing and making do by moving into land - in 1697 Thomas Willard bought *The Lawns* estate in Old Town. The landed nobility ruled, however, and Spencer Compton had *Compton Place* remodelled and enlarged by Colen Campbell over 1726-31.

Colen Campbell also built a flint folly, now the Belvedere on the Royal Eastbourne Golf Course by Paradise Drive, a fine and expensive example of the use of flintwork. Flints were silicates taken up by sponges in the chalk. This close-up shows knapped and squared flints.

With post-1688 stability and farming doing well the 1700s saw an upsurge in mobility, as the nobs with time and money to spare tried out this new idea of travel improving the mind. Spencer Compton, a politician of national standing in residence, also attracted those of the same class to Eastbourne, especially as the Downs made for easy riding. In 1713 Macky wrote, 'I lay at a pretty village called Eastborn and supped upon some little birds called Whit-ears. This village lies under the promontory so famous for the Loss of Ships, called Beachy Head'.

Macky refers to Beachy Head's reputation, and to the coast-hugging mariner of old the Beachy Head cliffs were fearsome. The erratic winds and rocky ledges meant hundreds of **shipwrecks** off the headland.

The earliest name we have is the *Marie* of Santander in 1368, but most went unrecorded, or appeared in the Parish Registers under, 'Burial of seaman washed ashore at Beechy'. There was also harrying of ships and the Eastbourne populace lined up along the Beachy Head cliff in 1778 to watch the *Greyhound* see off a French cutter attempting to ensnare colliers.

Remains of the *Nympha Americana,* a Spanish prize of 800 tons and 60 guns wrecked near Birling Gap on 29 November 1747. Whilst many wrecks went unnoticed, if there was something special, such as lots of gold and silver, the news spread and people came 'just to view' from miles away. It was effectively the car boot sale of the year.

Another visitor, the Revd Dr Richard Pococke, wrote in 1754, 'I went to the seahouses near East Bourne, and the people resort here to bathe and drink the sea water. The sea cliffs here are high and very fine springs of water run out of them'.

The town was also producing its own sons of note. John Hamilton Mortimer ARA, born in the High Street in 1740, misspent a wild youth painting legendary scenes and this self portrait.

**Sea bathing** developed from the practice of touring curative spas. The aristocrats who flocked to spas for a change of air and to recover from their excesses, wanted a new experience so sea bathing started at Scarborough in 1735. Dr Richard Russell gave the south coast a tremendous fillip with his book extolling the value of sea water to 'preserve health and cure many diseases'. Men bathed naked until Victorian times when stockinette costumes 'covering but not hiding the figure' made an entrance. Segregated bathing, however, lasted into the 20th century.

It must be understood that this bathing lark was not a pleasurable pursuit, but a medicinal need, the sea water was for drinking. It might have done some good too by flushing all the food adulterants and excess alcohol out of the system.

The locals vied to satisfy the visitors' other demands. Cooper's brewery started as Chapman's about 1749, and William Hurst founded the Old Town Brewery in 1777, which lasted, as The Star Brewery, into the 1960s.

**Fishing** was always a minority line in Eastbourne, but the fishing family of Erridge dates back to 1296. The name continues in the town, and for the November 1902 rescue of ss *Southport* no less than eight Erridges were members of the lifeboat crew. Another fishing family, the Hides, can trace their ancestors back to the 1500s. The fisher folk lived mainly at Seahouses, near today's Leaf Hall.

The *Lamb Inn,* Eastbourne's oldest hostelry, had rendered walls from Georgian times to 1912, when, after damage, the exterior was stripped to reveal the half-timbering of today. Both the Star and the Lamb were resting places for mendicant friars and pilgrims, and it is said - without much evidence - that there were tunnels for smuggled goods. Along with the *New Inn,* the *Lamb* was the starting point for the London coach as well as where the Fifth of November bonfires were held.

William Hickey provides a picture of 1776 Eastbourne. He and three companions were ferried ashore to Seahouses after a stormy channel trip. He comments, 'The boatman conducted us to a miserable looking dwelling where we expected neither victuals, nor drink'. When they went inside, however, 'The landlady had a blazing fire going in a clean room, and we sat down to as fine a dish of fish as ever seen at Billingsgate, with excellent sauces, followed by a pair of chickens washed down with ale, and finished with cheese. A casual enquiry revealed that the landlady did have some wine "which might not be good enough for gentlemen of quality", nevertheless a bottle was pronounced, "...as high-flavoured a claret as any in my own cellar", and each of us drank two bottles.

'The bill came to six shillings, "And what are we to pay for the drink?" "Oh I make no charge for that. Now and then, my boys run over to Guernsey on business and bring home a few dozen bottles". We ascertained that 'her boys' were smugglers and with considerable difficulty prevailed upon her to accept a guinea for as excellent a repast as four hungry fellows had ever sat down to.'

For hundreds of years **smuggling** was a way of life, and death - a Riding officer was killed at Langney as early as 1717. A Custom House was situated at Seahouses to the west of the present Ordnance Yard, and Excise officials (a separate service) operated alongside the Customs men from the 17th century, probably using the warehouse known to have stood in Church Street on the site of Edgmond Church.

Most of Britain's tobacco was smuggled, and nearby Crowlink was the conduit of so much smuggled gin that Crowlink *Geneva* was peddled around London. The unknown artist of this painting has depicted a landing at Cow Gap, just west of Eastbourne, onto horses and wagons.

A report of 13 June 1774, states, 'The officers of the customs went with five Dragoons to the seashore, but 100 smugglers rode up, fired shots at the customs officers, and disarmed them before loading the goods on above 100 horses'. A letter of 2 March 1784 says, 'Yesterday evening two cutters from the continent landed their cargoes here, which was conveyed away by men with horses.'

Smuggling, however, wasn't the romantic escapade so often portrayed. The smugglers, threatened with hanging or transportation, were ruthless ruffians with little regard for life and property. In the last sizeable Eastbourne episode in 1833 a Coastguard was shot dead by the smugglers near the Wish Tower.

The house opposite the *Lamb Inn* in the High Street was built by the Revd Dr Henry Lushington over 1776/7. A son sold it to Charles Gilbert in 1792, five years later it became the Gildredge-Gilbert Manor House, seen here c.1880. In 1923 it became the Towner Art Gallery, which is due to vacate the site 2005.

Such activities are largely in the past, but many visitors remain unaware of Old Town's ancient attractions. Apart from one of the oldest churches in the diocese, there is *Pilgrims*, a 13/14th century guild house; a medieval dovecote; and the *Lamb*, possibly of 14th century date and one of the oldest inns in the county.

Eastbourne was also a town of **windmills**. The mill mentioned in the Domesday Book was a watermill, almost certainly the one on the Bourne near the old Drill Hall in The Goffs. It stopped working in 1816 and nothing remains except for a fragment of French millstone that was rescued a few years back.

After windmills developed around 1300, there were 17 in the town at one time, mainly on the windy ridges of Ocklynge and Willingdon, with eight along St Anne's Road and Mill Road. Pashley Down had two, and the Mortimer family were prominent in the reintroduction of horizontal mills, with three in the town.

Although none are left in Eastbourne, two are well preserved at nearby Stone Cross and Polegate.

The last windmill was St John's Mill or Hurst's Mill in Mill Road, used until 1917 when the cap jammed. Most of it was demolished in 1950, and the vestiges went when flats were built on the site in 1986. Lawrence Stevens rescued the remains of the last millstone, which were incorporated into the boundary wall.

Millers weren't popular, for everyone thought that they cheated by keeping back some corn, a serious matter when conditions for the lower orders were harsh, especially if it had been a bad harvest. In 1651 the Church Registers recorded 'Thomas Buckle, a poor man, died of starvation.'

In 1780, however, the town had its first break, and no day-trippers either, but Royals. Yes, with sea bathing in fashion, with Royal patronage, and eventually, the railway, Hickey's 'miserable-looking' seafront was to experience a transformation. Many years after his visit William Hickey was to write, 'Eastbourne, only insignificant ... scattered houses in August 1776, has since become a fashionable place of resort'.

# 2. The conquering hero comes 1780-1849

Eastbourne's rosier future began when in June 1780 a Royal party came to the town and stayed into October, a sure portent that the town was on the up.

The Royals consisted of 12-year-old Prince Edward, Princesses Elizabeth, 10, Sophia, 3, and the baby Prince Octavius. Edward was to become the father of Queen Victoria and had Prince Edward Island in Canada named after him. They were accompanied by a governess, tutors and a chaplain.

The Round House, where Prince Edward stayed in 1780, and to the right the Field House, both just to the NE of the present pier. This painting represents the scene c.1840, just before the Round House, an old mill, fell into the sea.

The visitors had plenty to do. Apart from lessons, there was 'the Sea-Houses beach, where you enjoy sea air, bathing, the sands, sailing, shooting, hunting, walking and riding.' If the sea was chilly the Royal children bathed at Mary Webb's newly opened Warm Sea Water Baths - where the Leaf Hall is now. They also visited *Compton Place,* and went to nearby East Dean, Birling Gap, and 'did' both Herstmonceux and Pevensey Castles.

The Royal visit was at the instigation of James Royer, a Court Treasury official, whose Eastbourne house lay close to Susans Farmhouse, whence comes Susans Road. He also published the first *Guide to Eastbourne* in 1787 which described, 'the various beautiful prospects and diversified scenes of this healthy and romantic spot'. The Revd John Fisher, principal overseer of Prince Edward's education, accompanied the party and arranged sketching for the older children. Typical of Eastbourne's visitors, it was a family holiday lasting over the season.

A successful Royal holiday couldn't have done Royer's reputation any harm at court, and Fisher family members were Vicars of Eastbourne from 1779 to 1805.

Robert Gibbs, the *Compton Place* bailiff, wrote, '… every house is full and if ever this becomes a public place it will be more due to the Royal Children … than any other thing'. Indubitably the Royal visit put Eastbourne on the map.

Since then Eastbourne has had its moments, but has never looked back. Yet another Royal, Princess Amelia, visited the town in 1789 and 1790, so the 1780 visit must have been a great success - like all Eastbourne holidays.

Lady Elizabeth Compton Peters (1760-1835) was a descendant of Spencer Compton and the only child of the Earl of Northampton, who died of TB. Her marriage to Lord George Augustus Henry Cavendish, a son of the 4th Duke of Devonshire, on 27 February 1782 brought her Sussex estates into the Cavendish family. The couple weren't expected to inherit the title, but a grandchild, William, 2nd Earl of Burlington, became the 7th Duke of Devonshire.

Divertissements were now required to amuse the visiting gentry, and Fisher's Library appeared in 1794. A private school 'for the sons of gentlemen' was next when The Gables in Church Street [on the Edgmond Church car park] opened in 1790 - and ran until 1902. The curriculum was described as 'very little history or geography, but plenty of Latin and Greek', and the food was 'terrible'. To provide entertainment as well as instruction a South Street theatre opened in 1798.

Eastbourne-on-Sea's valuable publicity was continued by the impact of the French wars. First a new sort of visitor hove into sight; French courtesans fleeing from the guillotine. On one day in September 1792 over 300 émigrés put ashore at Eastbourne, and when the French wars started the next year and dragged on and off for over 20 years the little town became even busier.

Next an Admiralty Signalling station appeared on Beachy Head, and the threat of invasion demanded an influx of troops to guard the coast; one mad Frenchman had even proposed to attack via a tunnel under the Channel. At first soldiers were billeted in inns or tents, but there were insufficient inns to cope, and the men suffered so badly in camps that the building of winter quarters became essential. The *Sussex Weekly Advertiser [SWA]* of 2 June 1794 has mention of a barracks, and Ann Hudson states, 'July, Cavalry barracks for 54 men ordered and preparing to build', this was on the Letheren Place site, in Church Street.

Other barracks were erected east of the town in Langney, and in 1795 the East and West Langney Forts were constructed on a low bar of shingle, the Crumbles.

In 1802 the three joint Lords of the Manor of Eastbourne, Lord George Cavendish, Charles Gilbert and Inigo Thomas, leased an area of shingle to the Board of Ordnance; and this is the present TA Ordnance Yard in Seaside.

A crucial year was 1804. England was in danger of invasion, the bulk of the army was abroad, and home defence was partly in the hands of Militia raised around the country. For Eastbourne, however, the military presence boosted its size and importance. It was reported, 'in spite of the menace of the enemy, this little watering place has to boast of its fullest season ever known'. A letter from Eastbourne implies that romance conquers all, '...had a ball last night at the *Lamb Inn*, among many present was the beautiful Miss Vidler the best dancer I ever saw'.

An engineer, Captain William Henry Ford, drew up plans for the defence of the south coast, and in the spring of 1805 Brigadier-General William Twiss, an expert in defence works, selected the Martello tower sites, named after a Corsican fort. The SWA reported that on 9 September, 'Mr. Pitt and Lord Castlereagh were on Tuesday at Eastbourne ... and viewed with attention the Martello Tower erecting there'. Building continued until 1812, long after the threat of invasion had ceased in August 1805 when Napoleon broke camp at Boulogne to deal with Austria.

Part of the line of Martello Towers sited to protect the flat coastline between Eastbourne and Pevensey. The Great Redoubt Fortress, in Royal Parade Eastbourne, was built to act as a fort and depôt for the towers. Among later uses, the fort and some of the towers were brought back into active service during the 1939-45 war.

Martello Towers are still prominent along the south coast and have even been converted into residences, but of the towers built to provide covering fire over the low ground between Pevensey Bay and Beachy Head only six remain, and many are in poor condition. Number 60 survives, 61 is in the Martello estate, 62 is in a caravan site, 64 is on the sea edge, and 66 is near the new Sovereign Harbour. The one on St Anthony's Hill, 68, was demolished for housing although the site can be discerned by the arrangement of the roads. Number 73, on the Eastbourne seafront opposite Wilmington Square, is known as the Wish Tower. Built on a greensand outcrop, it owes its name to the marshy land, The Wish, near the outflow of a stream by the seafront. Its latest use is as a Puppetry Museum.

Nelson's victory at Trafalgar, in October 1805, removed all danger to Britain, and soon troops were taking the war to the French in Portugal and Spain. Not without losses, inevitably, and Major the Hon. George Cavendish, son of Lord George Cavendish, and our Lady Compton, of *Compton Place* was lost at sea returning from the Corunna evacuation in January 1809.

Possibly because of all these momentous happenings Eastbourne had been made a Post Town by 1797, beforehand letters had to be sent to Lewes to join the General Post. The place for receipt and dispatch of letters was in Old Town, and on 27 April 1806 Thomas How was appointed the first sub-postmaster.

The Vicar of Eastbourne from 1809, the Revd Dr Alexander Brodie, a scion of a Scottish family, who had made their money in Antigua, pressed for a better poor school instead of the room at St Mary's Parish Church, Eastbourne's earliest.

In 1814 the joint Lords of the Manor bought a plot of land opposite the church for a new St Mary's Church of England National School. Two years later the Gilbert family, probably Mary Ann Gilbert (right) added a floor enabling girls to be taught upstairs. The building became St Mary's Girls' School, and in 1952 a Girls' Council School, until demolition. The site is now part of St Mary's Court, the pupils having moved to Ocklynge Junior School in Victoria Drive, where the old school bell is kept.

The Revd Brodie bought Gore Farmhouse in 1810, 'Gore' meaning a triangular or awkward piece of land. The family weren't short of a penny, Brodie's wife Anna being the daughter of John Walter, the founder of *The Daily Universal Examiner* or *The Times,* and they added to the house, extended the grounds, and lived there until 1892. The site gave its name to Gore Park Avenue and Road.

A new £450 peal of bells was first rung on 26 October 1818, and they are the bells we hear today. The bill wasn't paid for two years. There would have been a ring of bells at the Parish Church from the time the tower was built. With the introduction of change ringing the need was for more easily handled bells and in 1650 the bells were melted down and recast.

Distinguished visitors were beginning to replace the army, and although not in sufficient numbers yet to compensate financially, they were welcome. William Wilberforce enjoyed a break with his family in 1808, the year after the success of his anti-slavery campaign in Britain, while Charles Lamb, the essayist, applied his usual label when he visited a town and called it 'dullest Eastbourne'. About this time Jane Austen's associations reached their zenith when the distinguished author set Eastbourne as the location for her unfinished novel, *Sanditon.*

Smuggling peaked with the military commitments of the French wars and firmer measures were needed to control it. The Preventive Waterguard, an inshore force, was introduced in 1809 to support the Customs and Excise Services in the control of smuggling, and at Eastbourne they had a station west of the Redoubt with a boat and Watch House. The Waterguard was superseded by the Coast Blockade, a naval force hand-picked to combat smuggling. They established stations in 1818 along parts of the Kent and Sussex coast extending westwards to Seaford Head. The Eastbourne Watch House was built in 1819 on the shingle near the SW corner of the Ordnance Yard, together with a warehouse and boathouse.

While there are records of 300 smugglers gathering for a landing at Crowlink in 1822, the Coast Blockade was effective. By 1824 it covered the entire Sussex coast, and in 1828 seven men from Eastbourne were transported for smuggling.

In March 1831 the Coastguard took over as an anti-smuggling force, also assisting in life-saving and helping at rescues. They used the Watch House as accommodation for the Chief Officer and family, until it became unusable after a storm in 1857. This station moved eventually to Wartling Road. Coastguard stations were also established in Martello towers and at Holywell, Birling Gap, Crowlink and Cuckmere Haven.

With changes in the tax laws smuggling was no longer profitable and large-scale runs had to wait for more recent times for revival. In the 1880s Beachy Head station, hitherto a detachment of Birling Gap, took over from Holywell.

As soon as Napoleon was safely in St Helena the Dragoon cavalry barracks in Church Street was sold off to local landowners, who in 1817 leased it to the Eastbourne Overseers of the Poor for use as a parish Poor House. Other barracks buildings in the town were demolished over 1818-23.

By 1817 the library was run by John Heatherly. In his guidebook of 1819 *A description of Eastbourne and its environs,* he describes it as, '...a good library, delightfully situated facing the sea, with one of the best lodging houses above, daily papers each day. In the adjoining room is an excellent Billiard Table kept quite select for the use of gentlemen only'.

'Mad Jack Fuller' of Brightling provided the funds for Eastbourne's first lifeboat, an 8m [25ft] rowing boat of ten oars. The lifeboat station was established in 1822, next in line after Newhaven along this south coast, and two years before the national institution. Fuller might have been eccentric, but as an astute politician he knew the value of publicity; for when his lifeboat made its first rescue he had a medal struck - displaying his name and bust.

In nearby Ratton Inigo Freeman (later Inigo Freeman Thomas to conform with his father-in-law's will) lived with his second wife Lady Frances Brodrick and 14 children. He added wings to *Ratton Manor,* and created the Upper Plantation for Lady Frances to view from her boudoir, where presumably she spent much time.

Clearly he needed cash for in 1830 he sold his rights to the Crumbles, as well as his Eastbourne-Parker third interest in the Manor of Eastbourne, to the two other manorial lords, the Cavendishes, or Dukes of Devonshire, and the Davies Gilberts. By 1840 two-thirds of the parish, 2600 acres, was in Cavendish hands.

The Gilbert name changed when Charles and Susannah Gilbert both died childless in 1816, and the 'Gildredge/Gilbert' sub-manor passed to their niece Mary Ann Gilbert. In 1808 she had married Davies Giddy, MP, and President of the Royal

Society 1827-30, who changed his name to Davies Gilbert. They lived in the Manor House that became the Towner Art Gallery and History Museum.

In 1845 the title of Lord of the Great Manor of Bourne was resolved by drawing lots, won by John Davies Gilbert, son of Davies and Mary Ann.

At the other end of the social whirl, the common soldier was swiftly demobbed after Waterloo and, with no trade, became a heavy charge on the parish, so the ratepayers believed the only way to bring down the taxes, which soared in the 1820s, was to introduce 'reforms'. One outcome of the Poor Law Amendment Act of 1834 was the Eastbourne Union Workhouse which opened March 1835 in Church Street's old Dragoon barracks. One aim of the 1834 Act was to gather the parish poor into union workhouses, in the case of Eastbourne for 14 parishes from Seaford to Pevensey. The theory of spreading the load was not unreasonable as the costs and resources of each parish varied enormously, unfortunately - as we see today – the measures weren't fully funded and turned into a cost-cutting exercise. A harsh regime was soon in evidence to discourage use of the workhouse; in September 1835 the Master kept Henry Collins, George Hatfield and Samuel Collins on bread and water 'for such number of days he may think necessary'.

Water-colour of Old Town 1862 by Alicia Lewis. Towards the lower right is St Mary's Church, behind is the tower of the workhouse chapel and the long building behind that is the workhouse. The far Downs show the cleft of the Brighton road.

The regulations included strict separation of married men and women, which was bitterly resented. On 20 November 1835 George Whiteman, Clerk to the Guardians, wrote, '... a great disturbance in the Eastbourne workhouse. The married persons in the house appear to have conspired to prevent the separation of man and wife. The conduct of the parties has been most desperate: fortunately ... the Guardians have (by force) succeeded in getting two of the worst characters (men) into the blackhole, but the house continues in great confusion.'

When the Guardians were accused by ratepayers of spoiling the inmates they replied that, 'the beer is of a very indifferent quality indeed little better than water'.

For a few years there was a workhouse school at Seaford, as part of the Eastbourne Union, and there is a letter expressing a sentiment redolent of the times, '... this Board still entertain the opinion that the children in the Seaford School House should not be taught to write as they would otherwise be in a better situation than the children of a considerable number of the independent Agricultural Labourers in this Union'.

There is no doubt that Poor Relief costs were capped: but at what a cost to human dignity. Charles Dickens who created Mr Bumble, the workhouse Master in *Oliver Twist,* wrote, '… few anomalies in England are so horrible that the poor should creep in corners to die rather than fester and rot in such infamous places.'

Elsewhere Eastbourne continued to attract the better class of tourist. In 1831 Dickens himself came to see Augustus Egg, the artist, who had rented *Pilgrims*, the oldest house in Eastbourne, and Holman Hunt was said to be a later visitor.

Dr Brodie died in 1828 after falling from his carriage in Ocklynge. His successor, the Revd Thomas Pitman, realised that there was a need for a church to cope with the increasing numbers living nearer the sea. He persuaded the Earl of Burlington to donate a site and Pitman raised the cash for what became in 1847 Holy Trinity Church (right).

The town appeared once more on the printed page. Theodore Edward Hook, who started the journal *John Bull,* had a character in his book *Jack Brag* (1836) amuse himself at Eastbourne by 'strolling on the sands, watching girls and throwing stones into the sea'. Truly there wasn't much else to do, for Eastbourne had stagnated since 1820. James Berry Morris wrote, 'In 1836 I journeyed from Lewes to Eastbourne in an old rumbling van occupying four hours on the road to spend my summer holidays.'

Fortunately, the first of our conquering heroes was on the way; for the coming of the railway was the beginning of Eastbourne as we know it. The line had reached Brighton in 1841, Lewes 1846, and by 1849 Polegate, from where Eastbourne passengers had to complete their journey by horse omnibus, horseback, or not unusually, on foot.

Until 1868 the town rail link wasn't directly connected to the outside world because a local train met the through Hastings train at Polegate station and, on a single track until 1862, shuttled between Eastbourne and Hailsham. Even so, the impact on the town was enormous.

One result was that in 1851 John Davies Gilbert constructed Terminus Road over farmland from the station to Seaside Road, linking up with Victoria Place (now part of Terminus Road) to give access to the seafront. Built for residential villas, it became the main shopping centre so needed widening in 1894 and 1898, but it was never the grand boulevard which the town required.

A modern commuter will readily believe that early railways were mainly concerned with the conveyance of goods rather than persons, but it was soon realised that coastal development would generate passenger traffic. The railways drove stage coaches out of business, the roads emptied of long-distance traffic, and coaching inns subsided into local pubs until resuscitated by the car in the 1930s.

Despite the Royal visit, and the influx of visitors during the Napoleonic wars, Eastbourne had changed little by 1840. The population was only about 3000, the stocks in Grove Road were in use for drunks, the nearest policeman was stationed at Pevensey, and farming was entering a period of depression.

Eastbourne's first train on 14 May 1849. The station to the right, a 7 x 4m. [20 x 12ft.] wooden hut, was in the middle of today's Terminus Road in front of the old Head Post Office. In the background is the *Gilbert Arms,* converted from the Hartfield Farmhouse, but known from the Gilbert's crest as *The Squirrel,* where crowds awaited the latest wonder of the age to the strains of a band playing *Behold the Conquering Hero Comes.* The day was spent on celebrations, winding up with a grand firework display.

Eastbourne's inaction between 1815 and 1840 was partly because the town suffered a loss of trade after the Napoleonic Wars, but also communications were poor, and the 6th Duke of Devonshire wasn't interested in developing the town.

Such delay was to the eventual advantage of the town, for the early developments had a rocky enough time as it was, and by the 1840s the local Cavendish, the Earl of Burlington, was taking an interest in the town.

The town was fortunate in that the two families, the Cavendishes and the Davies Gilberts, had vision, and were well served by their agents and trustees. It is thanks to their sage measures that Eastbourne owes much of its charm.

So by the 1850s, 70 years after the inaugural Royal Visit, Eastbourne was ready for controlled development.

# 3. Victorian Spring in Eastbourne 1850-1900

The coming of the railway to the sleepy village of Eastbourne 'certainly increased the prospects of the place considerably' as William, the 2nd Earl of Burlington, grandson of Elizabeth Compton, noted in his diary.

The Earl, a true Victorian, who became the 7th Duke of Devonshire in 1858, did his bit too. Over the next five years he invested £37 000 [some £2m today] to construct Eastbourne's first sea wall, and villas to entice the wealthy.

The Earl's first moves to implement the plans of his architect James Berry were not a success. The builders took up plots, the Grand Parade commenced in the spring of 1851, and the sea end of Terminus Road and Cavendish Place were also started. Tenants, however, were not impressed and all the builders went bankrupt. The real impact came when the Earl tried to auction the buildings and there were no takers, but no doubt many who 'told you so'.

The architect's concept of the Grand Parade in 1851, looking west. The spire of Holy Trinity Church can just be discerned on the right. The 'Carpet Gardens' of a sort date from the 1850s.

Grand Parade today. By 1938 the *Burlington Hotel* occupied the main part including the entire west end. In 1923 No. 5 became the *Claremont Hotel* which occupied the eastern end by 1951.

The original 'Marine Parade' commenced just by the *Albion Hotel* and ended at the *Round House* near today's pier. It was barely above the beach, and was constantly washed by the sea. Berry built his new Marine Parade sea wall using blocks of greensand found on the spot, but they weren't hard enough to bear the pounding. You can make out a few of the blocks just west of the pier.

Berry also tidied up Motcombe pond, Eastbourne's water supply. Again a more radical approach was needed to cope with the requirements, so the new Duke of Devonshire got rid of Berry and formed the Eastbourne Waterworks Company. This led to the appearance of George Ambrose Wallis as engineer to the Water Company. He erected a pumping station at the Bedford well in 1859, and with wells and headings at Waterworks Road this supply coped until the 1890s.

Henry Currey, the new Agent for the Duke, produced a comprehensive plan for the Duke's estate in 1859. This included Meads, which with the Duke's money and support would become the best designed seaside resort in England.

One long-standing Eastbourne family who did well with the changes were the Bradfords. Henry Bradford had established himself as a coal merchant in 1828 with wharves and yards at Seahouses where the colliers ran up the beach to discharge.

Samuel, one of his sons, realising that the railway would revolutionise the movement of goods, arranged to have a presence at the station from the beginning. At their peak Bradfords had 104 rail wagons, moved over 500 tons of coal a week, and supplied everyone.

The first builders might have had their fingers burnt, but others moved in. There was Edward Maynard, builder of *Kinburn House,* another was James Peerless whose building firm started in 1850 and continued, latterly as Peerless Dennis, into the 1930s. One citizen who had his fingers in everything was solicitor John Henry Campion Coles.

You can find the name of Ebenezer Morris, ironfounder, who came from Lewes, on most of the lampposts, gutters, manhole covers, railings (and, as on the right, coal hole covers) installed in Eastbourne between the 1850s and 1910.

Eastbourne elected a new Local Board to replace the Vestry, which had run the place for centuries. To record all this activity and perhaps puncture some of the pomposity the *Eastbourne Gazette,* the town's first newspaper, appeared on 11 July 1859. The *Eastbourne Chronicle,* which became the *Herald,* appeared in 1865.

The town's fathers realised that industry grime would repel the desired wealthy residents, but Eastbourne's continued growth relied upon competent water, gas, and later electricity, services for its residents and visitors. All dependent on coal, which the railway could supply. The London Brighton and South Coast Railway [LB&SCR] offered the Eastbourne Gas Co. a station site for a nominal sum if the gas company imported all its coal by rail.

Before the railway, coal came to Eastbourne by collier brigs. They were vessels of 50-100 tons with names such as *Bee, Collingwood, Pelican, Tally Ho* and *Tryall.* They were at their peak about 1850 but gradually they were supplanted, perhaps all to the good for they were notoriously unseaworthy.

One of Eastbourne's acceptable 'industries' was the private school. An early one was started in the 1850s by the Shoosmith family at The Grove, and only closed in 1896 to make way for Grove Road.

In spite of some uncertain spells the town was entering a period of rapid growth. The population doubled every ten years, and the town 'built by gentlemen for gentlemen' offered opportunities for traders who aimed their wares at those with money and time to spend.

Stephen Bindon started his furniture business in 1860 at Pevensey Road. It quickly became the most exclusive shop in the town, even supplying bedding to *Compton Place* for a visit of the Prince of Wales, later King Edward VII. The same year Richard Francis took over a branch of Parson's stonemasons, and soon had his own Carrara railway sidings. One business that carries on since its establishment in 1863 is Leonard Stevens, saddlers, in Crown Street.

Henry Evenden (1833-93) set up shop with John Terry as draper and silk merchant at the corner of South Street and Chiswick Place, now Memorial Square. The shop became Dickinson & French and is now the furnishers David Salmon.

Caleb Diplock's Lion Steam Brewery was perhaps the most successful venture. He came to Eastbourne in 1856, buying a house in Terminus Road which he called *London House,* in 1858 he bought the *Commercial Hotel [Diplock's Hotel],* and in 1863 opened his Brewery and Malt House. His brewery was well and truly christened with a supper and some 20 toasts to those involved in the building work. It seems only fitting that one of the last toasts was to the 'Foreman plasterer'.

He built Southdown Hall in Polegate, sold the Brewery and retired in 1883 with 'a noble fortune'; it didn't do him much good for he died the next year.

The original Marine Parade library was taken over in 1857 by Frederick and Elizabeth Hopkins. He was a cousin of Gerard Manley Hopkins, and a recognised amateur scientist, but died from scarlet fever shortly after their only child, Frederick Gowland Hopkins, was born so Elizabeth's brother, Thomas Stafford Gowland, came to run the shop. He went on to publish Gowland's Directories.

Of the new trades, Eastbourne's first photographer was Albert Vidler in 1861, working from South Street, he wasn't a success and went back to his day job of surveying. George and Rebecca Lavis became the best known Eastbourne photographers, although TB Rowe took most of their pictures.

With unbridled expansion there is always someone who goes too far. Thomas Hopley set up a school at 22 Grand Parade for the sons of gentlemen. There were only six pupils, all with special needs, and on 21 April 1860 Reginald Cancellor, 14, a backward lad with 'bad habits', was called to Hopley's study following 'intransigence' and beaten for two hours. The next morning the boy was found dead, but the inquest verdict was natural causes. The boy's brother came to Eastbourne, saw bruises on the body, demanded a post mortem, and when this showed horrifying injuries Hopley was arrested, found guilty of manslaughter, and jailed for four years. At the trial the Lord Chief Justice laid down that any parent or schoolmaster had a right to beat a boy, but in moderation and never in anger.

In 1861 Drs William Abbot Smith and Charles Hayman wrote a booklet

*Eastbourne a resort for invalids,* and after Drs DJ Hall and Hayman had proffered advice on the need for decent drains, the first sewage outfall at Langney Point came about in 1867. It was not one of Wallis' successes and needed modifying.

Soon after the rail station opened it had been realised that it was cramped and in the wrong place. The Davies Gilberts wished to open up their estate by constructing a new approach, Upperton Road, to by-pass Old Town with its narrow roads, steep hills and awkward corners. The station, however, lay in the middle of the projected route so in 1866 it was moved and rebuilt on much the same site as now. The Avenue, the jewel of the Davies Gilbert Estate, was laid out by Nicholas Whitley, and in 1904 Whitley Bridge was named after him and his son, Michell.

Frederick Gowland Hopkins OM (1861-1947). Born in Eastbourne, he watched the pier being built and cherished the hope that he could be involved in some great enterprise. He inherited his father's love of science and was Professor of Biochemistry at Cambridge from 1914, knighted in 1925 and President of the Royal Society 1930-35. In 1929 he became a Nobel Laureate for his work on accessory food factors now called vitamins.

It was also obvious that the Gas Company needed to move from its cramped station site to Lottbridge Drove, already connected to the Ballast Line, but the haggling over the costings went on until 1869. By now rail was essential not only to bring in coal, but also to dispatch the by-products, such as creosote and coke.

One of the first locals to achieve success was Henry Sutton. The family were bootmakers, but in 1861 he became manager of the *Railway Hotel* on the Terminus Road and Cornfield Road corner. The building of Upperton Road meant that the *Gilbert Arms* (or *The Squirrel*) had to be demolished and Sutton, an astute businessman sensing an opportunity, acquired a plot near the new station and built the *Gildredge Hotel* to which the Gilbert licence was transferred in 1870.

Sport and leisure were not forgotten. There was a Race Course on Bullock Down, and boating was a popular Victorian pastime. Eastbourne's Regatta was first held on 26 August 1859, and it became an annual event. The first recorded cricket match was in 1738, probably on the Links, near Eastbourne College's all-weather pitch today. From 1858 the Marsh Field, alongside the railway by the Ashford Road NCP, was the main venue. This was the scene of the visit of WG Grace in 1868, and of the first touring team, the Aboriginals, who got as good as they gave by giving a demonstration of boomerang throwing.

On 6 June 1865 our Dr Hayman proposed a 'Proprietary College to Educate the Sons of Noblemen and Gentlemen'. With the Duke's support, on 20 August 1867 Eastbourne College in Spencer Road admitted 15 boys under the Revd James Russell Wood as headmaster.

Church building strove to cope with the influx of people, and the church of (now) St Saviour and St Peter in South Street is accepted as the finest Victorian church in the town, with the graceful broach spire at 176 ft. [53m.] the loftiest. Perhaps appropriately it has always been known as a 'high church'.

St Saviour's was designed by GE Street in Gothic style, on a site given, as usual, by the Duke of Devonshire. The foundation stone was laid in a turnip field on 17 October 1865. Built, also as usual, by James Peerless, the £20 000 cost was borne by G Whelpton, of Whelpton's Pills; for some reason his son and grandson were the first two vicars. A purpose-built hall by DA Clarke was erected in 1957.

The wealth generated by Whelpton's Pills is an example, along with Holloway's Potions and Beecham's Powders, of how well the purveyors of useless 'restoratives' fared in Victorian times.

On 29 May 1867 Father Charles Patrick King took up his pastoral duties. There were only half-a-dozen Catholics in the town, and he held services in the basement of his house in Ceylon Place until in 1869 he built Stella Maris church for £450.

The same year Emma Brodie, daughter of the ex-vicar, persuaded the Duke to give £1000 towards the cost of St John the Evangelist church in Meads, and who built it? Why, James Peerless, of course.

In the 20 years from 1871 the population trebled from 11 000 and Eastbourne joined up with Meads. It was said of Meads in 1890, 'meadows and cornfields have become studded with stately villas and beautiful gardens', and in 1904 the *Eastbourne Chronicle* referred to it as, 'the unrivalled Belgravia of a salubrious and flourishing health resort'.

Not far from 'Belgravia' was Eastbourne's workhouse, hardly salubrious but flourishing after a fashion. The lines, *It is Christmas day in the Workhouse,* were by George Robert Sims, a journalist, who had a house in the town, so perhaps Eastbourne's workhouse was *the* one.

Newspaper headlines today delight in rubbishing the latest dietary fashion, whereas the workhouse inmates were grateful for any scraps. Breakfast and supper menus for males in the 1880s amounted to 8oz [225g] of bread, and one pint of gruel. For females, and children over seven years of age, 6oz of bread and one pint [450ml] of gruel, and younger children 6oz bread and ½pint gruel. No doubt the gruel was near enough water to maintain a healthy fluid intake. Dinner made up for it. Males got half a pound of bread [225g] *and* 1½oz of cheese, while women gorged themselves on 6oz of bread and 1½oz of cheese, and children made do on 4oz bread and an ounce of cheese. Good Food Guides rated it 'monotonous'?

Eastbourne workhouse c.1890, formerly horse barracks, later part of St Mary's Hospital.

To go with their diet sheet the inmates were given a series of graduated exercises entitled 'A Schedule of Tasks of Work'. Males had to break 12cwt [600kg] of flints per day – so you can see the justification for positive bread discrimination. The able-bodied women had it easy; they just had to pick merely 2½lb [1.2kg] unbeaten oakum (ship's ropes) or 5lb beaten oakum a day, or 2lb and 4lb in the winter. If they wanted to have a cosy time they could opt for ten hours washing or scrubbing, as they watched the old folk keeping osteoporosis at bay by chopping wood for the fires.

Many workhouses introduced a starvation diet for nine days after delivery of single women as 'a deterrent against the use of the workhouse as a place to be confined'. It was said of the Eastbourne workhouse, 'erring women who have been driven to seek the cold shelter of the workhouse walls in their hour of need have been excluded from any participation in the trifling luxuries afforded to the inmates at the joyous season of Christmas'.

Children outside the workhouse fared little better. Although the government gave grants for the education of the poorer classes, the only elementary schooling in Eastbourne was at Church Schools. Such private generosity kept the rates down, but it was storing up trouble.

On a slightly different educational plane, Eastbourne College decided to move from its temporary quarters to land in Meads given by the Duke of Devonshire. *Larkfield House* became the headmaster's residence, and the purpose-built buildings of 1870 were Henry Currey's first major work in Eastbourne. The school grew, additions were made, but progress was slow until in 1888 the Revd Dr Charles Crowden came in with 90 new pupils.

Eastbourne Ladies' College, in Grassington Road in 1870, was Eastbourne's first purpose built girls' school. The building, demolished in 1987, had been taken over by Eastbourne College and renamed *Pennell House,* after an Old Boy *VC.*

Eastbourne needed a boat landing stage, so a Pier Company was registered on 3 April 1865 with £15000 capital. Above is the pier, opened in 1870 and completed by E Birch two years later. Notice there is not much in the way of theatres or entertainment arcades, it was sufficient to have a walk on the pier, and some visitors even felt a little queasy with that.

Below: the result of a gale on New Year's Day 1877 when the landward part was swept away. The replacement section was built slightly higher than the original and you can see where the sections joined up to this day.

Other schools were moving to this healthy town. Clifton House School was brought from Oxfordshire to South Street by the Revd Edward Crake in 1868. It flourished and moved to a site in The Avenue. After about 20 years Peter and Douglas Gilbert moved their school, Roborough, into the building, where Sir Alec Guinness was a pupil. This school lasted into the 1939-45 war.

In the days before antibiotics or aseptic surgery, when recovery from a broken leg or pneumonia entailed months of convalescence, any town boasting of its health-giving properties hosted a convalescent hospital. So Eastbourne was delighted when the All Saints' Convalescent Hospital, run by Anglican Sisters, opened in 1869 at Meads.

Anyone involved with the law had to travel to the Petty Sessions at Hailsham, until two local magistrates, Reginald Graham and Leonard Willard, inaugurated a weekly sitting in the Vestry Hall, and from 1887 in the Town Hall. After 1911 the town had its separate Bench in accord with the new County Borough status.

'A good many buildings are going on or will shortly begin', so the Duke of

Devonshire wrote tersely of Eastbourne in his 1873 diary. The *Cavendish Hotel* had opened, but no doubt he was referring to the Devonshire Park complex designed for 'high class recreation', as part of a scheme to extend the holiday season. The site, at the junction of Carlisle and College Roads, had been left empty because of its marshy nature, and the Devonshire Park and Baths Company was formed in 1874, the Duke providing the land and £16 000 for half the shares.

The Devonshire Swimming Baths opened in 1874. Built by GA Wallis, they were the largest heated salt-water baths in the country; the separate Ladies' and Gentlemen's baths being filled and emptied by the tidal rise and fall of the sea, and heated to 70°F [23C]. Quite an engineering feat, and swimmers liked the sea water, but it wasn't always replaced by the flow at each tide and tended to become algid.

The Floral Hall opened in 1875 and the Pavilion the next year, both designed by Henry Currey. The Winter Garden seated 2000, has a large dance floor, and continues to be used for concerts, balls, shows and receptions. In 1875 JC Plimpton, inventor of the roller skate, gave a demonstration to open a huge new skating rink which ran from indoors to the outside. Devonshire Park now had a music garden and facilities for cricket, tennis, racquets, roller skating, and cycling, and tennis championships have been staged there since the 19th century.

The Devonshire Park Theatre, also by Currey, opened in 1884 and is described by H Clunn as 'one of the finest on the south coast'. After a make over by Frank Matcham in 1903 it is delightfully ornate inside, and the Italianate towers house the fire escapes. The oriental-style Public Bar in Compton Street, with its onion domes, now named the *Buccaneer,* was built by the Devonshire Park Company in 1897, possibly to ape the Indian Pavilion bought in 1891.

The *Grand Hotel* in 1890. On 28 May 1875 William Earp, a builder, applied to build the *Grand Hotel* on King Edward's Parade, and he became the first manager, the architect was RK Blessley. When built there were six bathrooms for its 200 rooms.

For the *Queen's Hotel,* Marine Parade, which opened 1880, Henry Currey was back in favour. It was positioned to divide off the working class part of the town; for before 1939 it was said that no lady would walk east of the *Queen's Hotel.*

Two more and quite different schools were begun in the 1870s. Moira House, a Girls' Boarding & Day School, founded elsewhere in 1875 is going strong in Upper Carlisle Road. The non-conformist New College, which began in Spencer Road moved to Compton Place Road in 1888. After the closure of New College the buildings were taken over by Temple Grove School until 1936. Today they house the

Dental Practice Agency and other NHS administration offices.

All this action was covered by the *Eastbourne Gazette,* bought in 1873 by TR Beckett. His son, Arthur, started that fund of Sussex lore the *Sussex County Magazine* in 1926.

The bicycle was an important factor in female emancipation and when the Eastbourne Bicycle Club was formed in 1877 there were about 180 members including 30 ladies, and the club had a reputation as a matrimonial agency. The club prospered until 1939, but was wound up in 1991. Bicycling didn't do member and secretary John Niedermayer any harm for he died aged 96 in 1953.

With yet another orgy of church building the story went that Eastbourne had more church seats per head of the population than any other town. The results varied from the tin-built Immanuel Church in Hyde Road, later the WRVS Centre, to All Souls' Church, notable for its separate bell-tower.

'In order to assist those anxious to help themselves' the Eastbourne Temperance Building Society was incorporated in 1877, and in 1885 it was considered time to start an Artisans' Dwelling Company. The aim was to build 4- or 5-roomed cottages for letting to families at a rent equal to what they were paying for two substandard rooms.

All Souls' Church, set on an insula in Susans Road and constructed in Lombardo-Byzantine style with a free-standing campanile. Built on shingle, it is alleged that there is more of the church underground than above. It was paid for by Lady Victoria Wellesley, a kinswoman of the Duke of Wellington.

A Seaside coffee house, *Ye Rising Sun,* was opened in 1879 by Wilhelmina Brodie Hall as a 'boon to the working classes', but really to combat the drink. It was a success, lasting until 1924. Coffee stalls were also run by the Church of England Temperance Society, sites included 'Memorial Square', where one went on serving until 1940. Wilhelmina (1845-1939), a clever grand-daughter of the Revd Alexander Brodie, was the first Eastbourne female Guardian of the Poor in 1883 and she took a great interest in the natural history and meteorology of the town.

Electricity first illuminated the Floral Hall in 1881, 'like a miniature Crystal Palace, more the appearance of one of the enchanted palaces in The Arabian Nights'. That year the population reached 21 000 with less than 40% born in Eastbourne and over 50% coming from outside Sussex. The next year the Eastbourne Electric Light Company was formed and leased the old Bedfordwell water works, moving in 1884 to Junction Road. The town's first public electric lighting was seen on 4 September 1882, five hours before New York.

Visitors to the town included Karl Marx, the founder of international communism; however, when a plaque was put up to him it was torn down. Richard Blackmore, the *Lorna Doone* novelist, and Sir Rowland Hill, the advocate of the uniform prepaid postage rate, were other holidaymakers, and pianist and composer, William Sterndale Bennett, also came frequently. Among the schoolboys at Kent House School in Staveley Road was EM Forster.

Among those who came to view the sights was Edward Lear, artist and composer of limericks. He visited a number of times being a friend of the Lushington family, and he painted this icy view of Beachy Head.

The year 1883 was the town's coming of age. Eastbourne's Charter of Incorporation was granted on 16 June, elections followed on 1 November, and the first meeting of the Borough of Eastbourne was held eight days later. George Ambrose Wallis, the Duke's Agent and Eastbourne's Mr Fix-It, had respectability thrust upon him when elected the first Mayor.

The Theatre Royal (later Hippodrome) and the Princess Alice Hospital opened, as did Eastbourne's first telephone exchange in Grove Road. The *Albion Hotel* had number 1, which it carried into the 1900s. In 1895 telephones were installed in the Town Hall, Fire Stations and Police Stations, while the exchange, catering for over 100 subscribers, moved to the corner of Grove Road and Hyde Road. Installation cost £3.50 and a local call was 1d ['/2p]. New businesses were also starting up and one that has survived is Charlwood's the jewellers.

The year also saw Eastbourne's most famous lifeboat rescue. On 25 November a barque, the *New Brunswick,* was in distress near Birling Gap. Realising that the lifeboat could not make way in the teeth of a strong SSW gale, it was decided to haul the *William and Mary* overland some five miles to Birling Gap. At the Gap the boat was launched into a violent sea and, under coxswain Charlie 'Bones' Hide, rescued the ship's crew. A heroic rescue tainted by arguments about payments.

On 4 January 1884 in a dense fog unusual for Eastbourne, and no doubt ascribed to global cooling, the Mayor laid the keystone of the sea wall extension round the Redoubt. The fishermen were provided with a new fishing station east of the Redoubt, but the fishing families were already diversifying, for in 1884 W & W Erridge paid £20 a year for permission to place deckchairs on Grand Parade.

The Duke's Drive, Eastbourne.

Meanwhile, west of the pier, in the 1880s and early 90s, the 7th Duke of Devonshire was shaping the Parades and Dukes Drive at his own expense.

Robert Campbell's dining rooms in Compton Street started the concept of eating out, and with George Brown he formed the Eastbourne Scottish Pipe Band which celebrated its centenary in 1996. One unsuccessful venture was Eastbourne's Market, this opened in 1888 at Grove Road arcade, but was wound up in 1904.

The Eastbourne Parliamentary constituency was formed as a result of the 1885 Boundary Commission; previously Eastbourne was in the Sussex constituency.

Sport was burgeoning. The oldest surviving soccer club in the town, and probably in Sussex, was formed as 'Devonshire Park' and played its first match against Clifton House School on 26 October 1881. The club moved to *The Saffrons* when that opened and changed its name to 'Eastbourne Town' three years later.

*The Saffrons,* the sports ground along Meads Road, opened in 1886 together with Larkin's Field. The name comes from the crocus grown in nearby Saffron Gardens. Over the years the Sports Club has offered archery, athletics, bowls, cricket, croquet, football, hockey, squash, and table-tennis. The main pavilion of 1889 cost £600, and since modernised and expanded, has burnt down twice.

Golf came to Eastbourne in the summer of 1887, and the Royal Eastbourne Golf Club was granted its title in the October. It was the first club in the county, along with Seaford. The 9-hole course was laid out so as to interfere as little as possible with the Duke of Devonshire's sheep grazing tenancy. The following year an independent Ladies Club was formed and became the Royal Ladies Golf Club.

When Canon Thomas Pitman, the low church, autocratic Vicar of Eastbourne, died on 13 May 1890, aged 89, the town mourned and Eastbourne's shops closed.

Canon Pitman's death saved him from the financial pressures threatening church schools, and the riots when the Salvation Army moved into the town.

Eastbourne had become a centre of education, catering for the children of colonial administrators, although families would move to Eastbourne simply because of the choice of schools. Meads was the usual site, with so many villas suitable for conversion. It is often claimed that Eastbourne had 365 schools, but there is no evidence for such a number, even GF Chambers' claim of 200 in 1894 is an exaggeration. It is difficult to track down every school when many moved and changed names repeatedly, but in 1897, for example, there were some 82 schools.

Such schools, however, did not provide universal education for Eastbourne's children and, in an effort to save local taxes, little official effort was made to cope with the need, relying on subscriptions and private benefactions. Eastbourne was one of only two authorities in England and Wales that did not have a School Board.

Salvation Army band playing on Eastbourne front, c.1890. Part of the violence towards the Sally Army in the early 1890s, in which instruments were trampled, and uniforms torn, was a reaction against strangers coming into the county and changing the ways of a lifetime. At least Eastbourne, unlike Worthing, didn't have to call in the armed forces to restore order.

School Treats, at least, were annual highlights, when hundreds of schoolchildren would go to Pevensey by train. At the end of a day of games and tea, and exhausted teachers, each child was given a bun and an orange.

Although generous gifts of land and money by wealthy churchgoers provided 656 extra places, the growth of Eastbourne brought demands that were beyond the church finances. By the 1890s there was again a deficiency of school places in Eastbourne, and the town signally failed to comply with the Technical Instruction Act of 1889. The Borough Council even attempted their own form of Private Finance Initiative, setting up a private company to build schools.

The Education Act of 1902 took away the town's choice by abolishing School

Boards, making local authorities responsible for education, and giving scope for scholarships to grammar schools. The first year the education charge was on the rates it hit 3³/₄d [1¹/₂p] in the £1, with ratepayers complaining bitterly.

The population was 34 969 in 1891 and Eastbourne had moved from an agricultural economy to tourism and education. Apart from civic amenities, however, there was no industry to antagonise the visitors, but this did mean seasonal unemployment, and pockets of poverty. Further changes were likely after the 7th Duke died and his benevolent influence was lost.

Eastbourne's own Borough Police force appeared on 5 April 1891. Comprising one chief constable, two inspectors, six sergeants and 29 constables, the total salary bill was £2 870 per annum. The town had just two beadles before 1842, when PC Joseph Carter was appointed by the county as the sole Eastbourne policeman on an annual salary of £46.30; the total strength from the County reached 30 by 1890. Eastbourne's first policewoman, however, was not appointed until May 1921.

Town Hall, 2003. When opened in 1886 the tower by Gillett & Johnson had space for a four-dial clock and bells. It remained empty, delayed by the usual cost question, until at noon on 11 July 1892 the £700 Westminster chiming clock was started by the Mayor. The chimes are Cambridge quarters.

After a recession in the late 1880s, business boomed. Elliott's Stores, founded in 1885 by Herbert Elliott on the South Street and College Road corner, became the premier Eastbourne grocer. Residents always mention Elliott's coffee grinder and the wonderful aroma. Another high-class provisions' purveyor was Cave Austin.

Not so welcome was an Eastbourne smallpox epidemic between August and December 1895 with 15 cases and two deaths. This led to the building of a Smallpox Isolation Hospital on the Crumbles, near Martello Tower 65.

A typhoid outbreak that year led to greater changes. Eastbourne's water supply was not the direct cause, but for years people had complained about the town's discoloured and brackish water, due to over-pumping. As a result some old sources were opened up, such as Motcombe pond, known to be contaminated. Finally the Council told the Water Company that they would be taken over unless they invested in an adequate new source, and this led the company to open up the headings at Holywell and Friston that are part of Eastbourne's supply to this day.

Eastbourne held its popularity. An unexpected regular visitor until his death, also in 1895, was Friedrich Engels who collaborated with Karl Marx on the *Communist Manifesto*. When, as he wished, his ashes were scattered on Beachy Head, Karl Marx's widow was present. A contrasting life was George Ambrose Wallis. Agent for the Duke, he ran the Cavendish Estate, and his brother, William Lumb Wallis, most conveniently ran a building firm. GA Wallis' Devonshire Park Baths and the tiered Western Parades were incredible achievements in the days of spades and wheelbarrows. He built himself mansions: *Holywell Mount, The Links, Clovelly* and *Fairfield Court,* of which only *Clovelly* in Blackwater Road remains - converted into flats. Some say his death - again in 1895 - was just in time to save his reputation, but while he was probably involved in shady deals he was a brilliantly innovative civil engineer and capable manager.

In a step forward the next year, Mr JH Hardcastle was appointed Eastbourne's first Borough Librarian, and the Vestry Hall library, Grove Road, opened on 7 July.

The Queen's Diamond Jubilee in 1897 was a time of sports days and teas. The Eastbourne Bowling Club was founded and the Willingdon Golf Club at Ratton started with nine holes. The coup was the 1897-8 Mayoralty of the 8th Duke of Devonshire, a national figure.

Although the Parades and Upper Duke's Drive were finished and paid for, the 8th Duke, an astute politician – and womaniser - had to cut the family losses, which he did by withdrawing wholehearted financial support for commercial ventures, selling off unwanted land and putting the money into shares.

Thomas Henry Huxley FRS, biologist, resided in Staveley Road, Meads, over 1890-95. Darwin had needed a protagonist for his theory of evolution and Huxley wanted a cause, so he expounded the received form of Darwinism. He coined the term 'agnostic', as well. Charles Darwin had written part of *The Origin of Species* while on a 1850s holiday in Eastbourne at what is now Marine Parade.

Seaside resorts now had a life of their own with piers, promenades and Pierrot shows. Visitors had lost any Brontë romanticism and wanted an escape, and increasingly it was the middle and lower classes sampling the delights, such as young ladies sporting new 'healthy' corsets which by chance improved the figure.

Eastbourne-upon-Sea had been cradled by the railway and, despite recurrent over-ambitious property speculations, had grown faster than any other south coast town in the second half of the 19th century. By 1900 it was the largest town in Sussex after Brighton. Yes, the Earl of Burlington had been right, Eastbourne had increased its prospects considerably, and was the best yet to come?

# 4. Edwardian summer, and the aftermath 1900-39

On New Year's Day 1900 the Council bought the Eastbourne Electric Light Co. for £82 135. The company had 516 customers, but by 1933 the number was 14 400.

In 1901, however, the councillors turned down a proposal from the railway company to move their works from Brighton to Eastbourne. The thought was that a sooty invasion by railway workers would not enhance the town's image.

The Western Lawns opened in 1883 to a design by Henry Currey, and were conveyed to the Council in 1902 by the 8th Duke of Devonshire, whose 1910 bronze on granite statue stands in the centre. It was where the residents of Meads paraded to show off their finery, the Snoot Parade, and where the belles and beaux might eye each other up. As was the Duke's habit the statue has him with his pince-nez in his hand. It was also the custom after a riotous night at the *Grand Hotel* for some blade to plonk a chamber pot on the head of the statue.

Freeman Freeman-Thomas of Ratton Manor sold 82 acres to the Council for a new park at £3000 on condition that they built a road from Eastbourne to Ratton. The road was constructed by William Lumb Wallis for £10 211. The new park was named after Lord Hampden, grandfather of Freeman-Thomas and erstwhile Speaker of the House of Commons, and officially opened by Lord Rosebery on 12 August 1902, with guests driving in carriages and char-a-bancs along the new road, now Kings Drive after Edward VII. GT Scott provided the flowers; the photographs were by G&R Lavis, and Brufords made the ornate opening key.

In 1901 electric lighting for the pier was installed by Percy and Harry Caffyn. They had joined their father's gas business in 1892, but branched out into electrical appliances. Another Eastbourne family firm from that time was Walter Llewellyn & Sons. Walter and William Llewellyn started as jobbing builders in December 1899 and the firm celebrated its centenary with a £140m turnover, but was taken over by ROK in 2002.

The present pier theatre opened on 15 July 1901. A new bandstand was erected near the theatre and, in the middle of the pier, two games saloons were added. Apart from the 1100-seat auditorium the theatre contained offices, bars and tea-rooms. At the apex was a camera obscura, then the largest in the country. Betty Palmer says, "This was a large white disk, on which were focused views of Eastbourne. You could see people as far away as the Wish Tower as clear as clear".

The 'new' lighthouse being built at the foot of Beachy Head. The Belle Tout one had not proved satisfactory being obscured in misty conditions, but the new one reflected light off the white cliffs in all weathers. This shows the construction platform and the coffer dam around the base.

Nearing completion, the 720 Cornish granite blocks were shaped at the quarry. All the men, equipment, and materials went down via a cable car from the cliff top to the platform. Work started in 1899 and the oil lamp was first lit in October 1902.

The foundation stone of Our Lady of Ransom Church in Grange Road was laid 11 December 1900. Built by Mark Martin to a Late Decorated Gothic style by FA Walters in Bath stone, not ideal as it is affected by salt. The church was opened 15 December 1901 by Father Lynch in the presence of Bishop Bourne, and consecrated 8 July 1926, when all the debt had been settled.

Schools continued to appear. One that flourishes today was started in 1894 by Mrs Anna Browne as a preparatory school for Eastbourne College. She called it St Bede's after the recently canonised Venerable Bede. It did well and when she sold it in 1901 St Bede's began its independent existence in Duke's Drive. In the 1970s a senior school opened in the Dicker at Horatio Bottomley's old house.

Freeman Freeman-Thomas, who sold the Hampden Park land, was also landlord and first president of Willingdon Golf Club when it was extended to 18-holes in 1903. The clubhouse dates from the next year.

In 1900 Caffyn's electrical shop at 12 The Colonnade had been asked to store a car. Further requests to store cars – for no hotels had garages – convinced Percy Caffyn that the future lay in cars, although as he pointed out, "We didn't know what a garage was, we called it a coach house." Cars were first seen on Eastbourne's roads in May 1896, early Eastbourne registration letters were AP, and PN for East Sussex, predating the HC and JK for Eastbourne. The town's first motor taxi licence was issued to Mr H Strudwick in 1899; it was restricted to certain routes and the speed was not to exceed 5mph within the Borough. Speeds had increased by the time of Eastbourne's first motor fatality on 31 March 1904 when the young daughter of a local builder was knocked down in Upperton Road.

Clement Brewer moved to Eastbourne for health reasons and opened his shop in Cavendish Place in 1904. He mixed his own paints of white lead, turps and colours or whiting, and made up his own pattern books at a time when you had to trim wallpaper. Quality wallpapers were in demand in Eastbourne, at 4d - 9d a roll. His six sons came into the business, the eldest, Jack, joined 1910 and opened the Redhill branch. In the 1930s the range extended to doors, glass and board. The office was centralised after the war, and in 1947 the first grandchild, another Jack, joined and became chairman in 1975. The business now has over 100 branches.

The name Holywell was now applied to what had been a chalk pit at the far western end of the Parades. This was laid out as an Italian Garden in 1904-5 to provide work for the unemployed. It cost all of £400, which the Council had to borrow.

The town's first purpose-built public library opened on 28 July 1902 in Seaside. To keep the cost down to only £2188 the branch library had to be combined with the slipper baths, thus solving the problem of what to read in the bath. The baths were popular when most Seaside houses did not have a bath, and in April 1924 they were extended and the library moved along the road. The baths closed in 1976 and the premises were bought for £35 000 by the Eastbourne Operatic and Dramatic Society as rehearsal rooms.

Eastbourne badly needed a Central Library and a Technical College. At last, after the Duke gave the land in 1899 - the sites of the fire station, vestry hall and sheepwash – and Andrew Carnegie, the US oil and steel millionaire and philanthropist, and later Freeman of the Borough, contributed £10 000, the Duchess of Devonshire was able to open the Technical Institute on 8 August 1904.

In January the next year, Motcombe Swimming Baths in Old Town opened and later in the year Achille-Claude Debussy, the French composer, shocked the town by escaping from Paris to the *Grand Hotel* with his pregnant mistress. He completed *La Mer,* and wrote a few other pieces whilst in Eastbourne.

The Queen Alexandra's Cottage Homes, in Seaside, opened on 5 June 1906. Intended for 'the ageing and deserving poor', the rent was $1/2$p a week. Queen Alexandra personally insisted on maximum fire-proofing, and Princess Alexandra attended the Golden Jubilee. Over the years they have been extended and upgraded.

The *Links*, Meads Road, was a mansion built in 1869 and set in extensive grounds, now part of a housing development. The word 'links' means slopes of Downland and predates the golf course. It became a famous Ladies' School under Miss Jane Potts from 1908-25. The reason for her success was that Miss Potts, known as 'Potty' in Royal circles, had been governess for ten years to Princess Alice, Countess of Athlone (1883-1981) who sent her daughter, Lady May, to the school. This patronage assured the school of pupils such as Edwina Ashley (Lady Mountbatten), and Dame Felicity Hyde Peake, a Director of the WRAF 1949-50.

The Technical Institute was designed by PA Robson and cost £38 000. It held a Library, a Museum, and Technical, Continuation and Art Schools.

Eastbourne's private schools remained an essential part of the economy, providing work for gardeners, cooks and maids as well as teachers, and buying everything, from books to victuals, in the town. Elise Randall would say that she started her Eastbourne School of Domestic Economy in 1907 with one Meads' house, one girl and £5 in the bank. 'Ranny' was a character, she called everyone 'Darling', went everywhere on her bicycle, but Ranny's became a prestigious place.

The Royal Eastbourne Golf Club, now also most fashionable and of 18-holes, enlarged the course in 1904 and built a new clubhouse. The Prime Minister, AJ Balfour, was a member in the early 1900s.

Eastbourne's third major golf course was constructed on Davies Gilbert land to the west of the town in 1907/8, reflecting the success of the Royal and Willingdon clubs. Originally Eastbourne Artisans, it is now the Eastbourne Downs Club. The present clubhouse was completed in 1972, when the original became a Youth Hostel until it suffered an arson attack in 2003. Rebuilding commenced in 2004.

Another golf enthusiast was Alfred Ryder who ran a bookshop in South Street. He became captain of the Eastbourne Downs Golf Club, having been barred from the Royal Eastbourne because he was in trade. Alfred's son, Thomas, won a scholarship to Eastbourne College who lifted their 'ban' on the sons of tradesmen specifically for him. An outstanding sportsman, Thomas won the *MC* in 1918, became an accountant and his sons were pupils at St Cyprian's Prep. School.

This famous school had moved to new buildings in Summerdown Road in 1906. The redoubtable headmaster and wife were Mr & Mrs Vaughan Wilkes, it was, however, Mrs Wilkes' presence that dominated the school.

St Cyprians' many famous pupils, such as George Orwell and Cyril Connolly, clearly had almost one-to-one tuition in this schoolroom. The site is now Eastbourne College Memorial Playing fields in Paradise Drive.

She taught English, Scripture and History (the school won the Harrow History Prize several years running) and encouraged 'simplicity, honesty and avoidance of verbiage', qualities evident in the writings of her pupils. Eric Blair (George Orwell) won two scholarships from the school, and it is reputed that his *Animal Farm,* of 1945, was based on Willingdon. The school burnt down in May 1939, when one of the maids lost her life. It finally moved to Oxford.

Talking of fires, in 1884 Eastbourne's new Council established a Volunteer Fire Brigade, of which JA Hounsom, a volunteer, became Chief Fire Officer in 1897, and opened a new Fire Station in Grove Road at a cost of £6250 in 1905. The first motor fire engine was purchased in 1912 for £925. Not until Hounsom retired in 1931, was the Brigade reorganised, and DW Spence appointed as its first professional Chief Officer. Incredibly, the first fire engine to give the firemen protection from the elements was a £2225 Dennis Limousine of 1936.

Meads reached its zenith in Edwardian times. Until the 1939-45 war it remained a haven of exclusive homes inhabited by the wealthy with servants to care for the grand mansions and gardens. The residents were mainly upper crust with a sprinkling of retired colonials, military types, professionals and a few self-made. Before 1914 servants got up at four in the morning and time off was one evening a week and one day a month. George Meek, a local bathchairman, wrote a book on his hard and unrewarding work, with an introduction by HG Wells.

Spencer Compton, the 8th Duke of Devonshire, died in 1908. He left no legitimate children and his nephew, Victor Christian William (1868-1938) succeeded as the 9th Duke. Mayor of Eastbourne 1909-10, he proclaimed King George V from the Town Hall balcony to a crowded Grove Road on 9 May 1910.

The new Duke also sought ways of cutting expenses to cover death duties. He sold the Jevington Stud Farm and again offered Devonshire Park to the Council, this time for £110 665, but polls of electors in 1913 and 1914 were firmly against.

Moving pictures had been shown on the Pier in 1903, but the first public show was in the Constitutional Club's building about 1911 when the *Picture Palace* opened, to become the *Tivoli Cinema*. By 1915 the *Tivoli* had been joined by the *Eastern,* Seaside, the *Central,* Seaside Road, and the *Winter Gardens Cinema* in the Devonshire Pavilion. Apart from a few breaks, the *Tivoli* entertained Eastbourne residents and visitors until its final closure in 1982.

More evidence of new technology was Blériot's monoplane on display at the Devonshire Park a mere nine days after its epic channel crossing in July 1909. Eastbourne, however, had to wait until 19 April 1911 before a plane (crash)landed in the park. Was that to celebrate the census population of 52 542, or the Incorporation of the town as a County Borough on 1 April?

Eastbourne's Grand Parade, 1906. Apart from the parasols to keep the sun off, it shows the Birdcage Bandstand (1884-1934) and the Pier Theatre, opened in 1901.

Largely due to the initiative and drive of Frederick Bernard Fowler, who taught himself to fly on a Blériot monoplane, the town had its own Eastbourne Aviation Company [EAC] and airfield. Established in December 1911 it was just west of St Anthony's; a seaplane base followed at the Crumbles end of Lottbridge Drove.

With 2158 hours of sun in 1911 (not to be exceeded until 2003 with 2162 hours) tourism was boosted, and to cope with the demand, new suites had been built on the west wing of the *Grand Hotel.*

The first X-rays at the Princess Alice Hospital were taken in 1912, but the news that shook Eastbourne to its foundations that year was the October murder of Police Inspector A Walls.

A man was seen on a canopy above the door of 6 South Cliff Avenue and Walls, the seafront inspector and a year from retirement, went towards the man saying, "Come down old chap, do", whereupon the burglar lent down and shot him. Walls staggered into the roadway mortally wounded. The man charged, John Williams, alias George Seymour, was part of a criminal set. The investigation produced some period pieces: after the shooting, John/George and his girl Flo went to the *Picture Palace* to see *Dante's Inferno,* and the evidence included phrases such as, "I knew immediately he wasn't a gentleman". Thousands attended the funeral on 16 October, while Williams was found guilty and hanged the next year.

On 8 April 1913 phosphorus was posted in Eastbourne pillar boxes – the first evidence for suffragette activity in the town. Shocking, but nothing to the outrage when in May hassocks were set on fire at St Anne's Church, and *Votes, Votes, Votes* scratched on a religious painting. The town's record of suffragette action was lost with St Anne's in the 1939-45 war, along with a brass to the memory of a parishioner, Capt. Lawrence Oates, who walked out to his death in an Antarctic snowstorm rather than delay Capt. Falcon Scott and his comrades.

HG Wells (1866-1946) novelist and a lover of Rebecca West, among others, was a frequent visitor to the town, and took his first joy flight along the Eastbourne sea front.

Sir Ernest Shackleton (1874-1922) had family in the town and visited in 1914 just prior to his Antarctic expedition which included an epic sail in an open boat of 800 miles.

The next event of 1913 was the laying of the foundation stone of St Aidan's Methodist Church, Seaside. The name was a link with the vicar who was from Northumberland, as was St Aidan. The organ was pumped by hand for the first 34 years, but the reason why the walls of the church bulged and became unsafe was that it was built on beach shingle. It was demolished for sheltered housing in 2002.

The funeral of Carew Davies Gilbert in December 1913 was in an overflowing St Mary's Church. He had been Lord of the Manor of Eastbourne during the town's rapid development, and had donated to the town the Seaside Recreation Ground on the occasion of Queen Victoria's Golden Jubilee in 1887, the Gilbert Recreation ground (now Princes Park), and the land for St Anne's Church. Interment took place at East Dean, the coffin carried on a farm wagon from Eastbourne with eight bearers walking alongside dressed in smocks.

The same month Charles Jewell hosted a Christmas treat for 1000 poor children in the Floral Hall at Devonshire Park. Mr Jewell was a philanthropist who, having made his money in Argentine cattle ranches, retired to Silverdale Road, complaining of income tax at 2½%. He also raised funds for the Soldiers' and Sailors' Home in Upperton Road (which had been started by Flora McCartie in 1905 to teach a trade to disabled ex-servicemen) and he helped the families of wounded soldiers, the 'Blue Boys', in the 1914-18 war.

On 27 July 1914 Eastbourne's Tuberculosis [TB] Hospital opened at a cost of £2143, plus £1250 to the Davies Gilberts for the site. It was built at a remote edge of the town (now Bodmin Close) because TB was the plague of the age, deaths from it far exceeded cancer deaths, and of the first 1000 patients in the hospital 530 died, despite the open-air therapy when in winter snow would blow in over the bedclothes.

During a July 1914 visit by a squadron of the Home Fleet the sun shone on the 15 000 people who passed through the pier turnstiles to view the warships. The Sussex County Agricultural Show was held that month on fields near Summerdown Road, soon to be put to wartime uses.

Arthur Clarkson Rose, who worked with Olive Fox, appeared at Seaford over the summer of 1914 in his first concert party. Over the next 50 years there was seldom a Christmas pantomime without him, or a production of *Twinkle*, the name of his summer shows, but otherwise the Edwardian summer ended on 4 August 1914, when the Germans invaded Belgium, and the world was never the same.

It was acceptable that the Admiralty requisitioned Eastbourne's airfield as a Royal Naval Air Service [RNAS] base to train pilots, and that large houses in the town were taken over for Red Cross Hospitals to help cope with the scale of casualties. Genteel Eastbourne could even stand the sight of Lancashire Fusiliers drilling in Devonshire Place, but it was approaching the unacceptable to view off-duty soldiers squatting on the pavement playing the card game 'Brag' for money.

Eastbourne folk were satisfied that the town's main contribution to the war effort was the Summerdown Convalescent Camp; wooden huts on brick bases to hold 3500 wounded soldiers, so called 'Blue Boys' from their uniform.

Next the workhouse had to contribute to the war effort. The buildings were converted into the Eastbourne Central Military Hospital, for critically ill patients, with the first admitted January 1916. In all 16 000 were treated, including airmen from the 1917 Jevington airship crash, until it closed in July 1919.

A Cavalry Command Depôt also opened to bring healthy men up to the standard of fitness required for front line duty. The huts were sited on Corporation land now bounded by Beechy Avenue, Victoria Gardens and Victoria Drive.

Part of Summerdown Camp which offered rehabilitation, good food, and entertainment, 'varying from a dental clinic to a skittle alley'. Some 150 000 went through the camp, probably the largest of its sort in Europe, and over 90% returned to active service. In the background, you can make out the only two houses in Pashley Road at the time.

Apart from two residents winning *VCs,* Eastbourne contributed to the war effort in varied ways. The Bus Depôt went over to war production, and in addition Eastbourne College, Caffyn's Garages and Lovely's Garages made shell cases or assembled aircraft, and three battalions of local men came forward for the Royal Sussex Regiment as part of Lord Kitchener's appeal for 100 000 volunteers.

Eastbourne wasn't finished with hospitals. The 16th Canadian Base Hospital opened at All Saints in January 1917, mainly for Canadian units at Seaford. Later in

1917 a Catholic Order of nuns opened *Fernbank,* in Hartington Place, for wounded officers; it was to become *Esperance,* a private nursing home.

Otherwise the town went on much as usual. TS Eliot, poet, critic, dramatist and Nobel Laureate-to-be, spent his 1915 honeymoon in Eastbourne.

Jack Warne wrote, 'The war had not affected Eastbourne. Holidaymakers came as in peacetime, the *Grand Hotel's* receipts and profits rocketed, and the wounded soldiers at Summerdown Camp, and in the big houses converted into hospitals, were a tonic to the town. The 'Blue Boys' were a happy lot and they put on shows, such as pantomimes, sports days and galas, and I never associated them with the grim struggle in France until one day in 1917 when I joined a knot of people near the pier. The word bandied round was 'survivors' and shortly a group of sailors, bareheaded, barefooted, in bedraggled blue uniforms, came past the kiosks. They looked strained and exhausted and the crowd saw them pass in silence. It emerged that they were from *HMS Ariadne,* an 11 000-ton minelayer sunk six miles off Beachy Head, by U-65, with the loss of 33 lives.'

The Churchdale Road Depôt of Eastbourne Municipal Buses, now demolished for housing. During 1914-18 the bus workshops were on 'war work', when they assembled mines and produced some 370 000 mortar bombs.

Over 50 ships were sunk by U-boats off Eastbourne and Beachy Head, the first being the collier *Branksome Chine* sunk by U-8 on 23 February 1915, and the last recorded sinking was the trooper ss *Moldavia* in 1918, torpedoed by U-57. Fifty-six lives were lost, but they were almost the only casualties of two million Americans transported across the Channel.

Rationing meant residents needed no encouragement to work the allotments provided by the Corporation and Compton Estate. Another sign of the times, however, was the town's first Venereal Diseases clinic in 1917, discreetly housed in a hut at the rear of the Town Hall.

The Armistice in November the next year was greeted with thanksgiving, jubilation, and dancing on the Western Lawns. By May 1919 all the women employed to replace men had been discharged, and there were those who thought that the 1914 ways would return. For quite a few families a permanent gap would remain, Ocklynge cemetery has 130 war graves, and others are in Langney cemetery. Many survivors were scarred by their experiences, strong men being frightened by the sound of thunder or a sudden bang bringing back memories.

With the rest of the world, the town suffered from the influenza pandemic. Of the 191 Canadian graves in Seaford cemetery 114 were almost certainly influenza victims, 70 of whom died at All Saints' Hospital.

The Ordnance Yard Hospital, in Seaside, closed after 1918 along with the Red Cross hospitals and temporary camps, and the years just after the war were marked by auctions of items, from complete huts to pillowcases. In 1919 the Council purchased the huts at the Command Depôt for use as temporary housing, the first families moving in that summer. By 1923 there were 600 residents. These homes for heroes had no insulation, outside water taps and lavatories, and they were noisy, damp and cold. Mrs Sally Sands' parents started married life in *The Hutments*. Her father had been a patient in the Central Military Hospital, having been gassed. "He developed TB and died at 40". In 1920 the Council opened six of the huts as an Open Air School, at a time when rickets and bone TB were common. It became the Downs School in 1959 and continues for children with learning difficulties.

It is understandable why thousands attended on 10 November 1920 to see General Lord Horne as he unveiled Eastbourne's War Memorial in memory of the one in fifty residents who died in the war. Canon W Streatfeild conducted a short memorial service, and Sir Charles Harding, the deputy Mayor, but Mayor throughout the war, recited the contributions made by Eastbourne in his speech. The names of the fallen are carved on oak tablets kept in the Town Hall.

Those aspects of Eastbourne life most affected by conscription and requisitions, such as sport, orchestral music and education were slowly recovering. The 1920-21 football season was most successful for the Eastbourne Royal Engineers Old Comrades Club for they won the East Sussex Cup - when the first radio transmission of a sporting event was made from Eastbourne. In 1946 the club moved to the Princes Park Oval, where under the chairmanship of Alderman Percy Wood they raised funds to build a grandstand, and in 1952 the name was changed to Eastbourne United. The Eastbourne Men's Hockey Club was founded in 1919, even though there are references to men's hockey at Larkin's Field before 1900. Many girls' schools also played in the 1890s about the time the Hockey Association was formed, but Eastbourne's women's club wasn't formed until 1950.

After the war the Duke's orchestra merged with the Council's Municipal Orchestra, and Capt. Henry Amers emerged as conductor of the 35-piece Devonshire Park Orchestra, with a contract to provide a military band. This was the start of a fine record of orchestral and military band concerts which most people hope continues. Captain Amers was Eastbourne's Director of Music 1920-36, and from 1924 he conducted a Municipal Orchestra at the Winter Garden, which with a strength of 40, was the largest such orchestra in the country. Always impeccably dressed in a military style with belt and sash, Amers was an able and popular musician, however, his trim figure generated whispers that he wore a corset.

Education was getting back on course as well. The Revd Edwin Browne had turned the Colstocks Farmhouse school into St Andrew's, a successful preparatory school. *Eversley Court,* 14 St Anne's Road, Ascham School from 1893, until taken over by the RNAS, was bought by Eastbourne County Borough in 1919 for £13 733 to house the Boy's Grammar School. The next year the Municipal Girls' Secondary School moved into 5 Upperton Road, with their junior departments next door at number 7, *The Glen.* They were both large detached houses, dating from the 1860s.

Eastbourne County Borough purchased the next door house too, the old Red Cross Hospital, 9 Upperton Road, for £4179 from the Davies Gilbert family, opening it in 1920 as a Maternity Home, for married mothers only. With extensions it provided 25 beds, and over 20 000 babies were born there until closure in 1976. Until 1948 mothers paid £2.10 a week and stayed on average $17^1/_2$ days, enjoying the rest. Before 1918 there were no local District Midwives, instead each doctor who practised obstetrics had a 'handy woman', some handier than others.

The bus firms responded to another result of the war, namely, a demand for tours to the battlefields of northern France. By 1921 Chapman's were offering three tours a season. The vehicles had little luggage capacity and were so unreliable that a back-up vehicle was often used to carry petrol, spares and luggage.

What with the post-war social upheavals Eastbourne could have done without two grisly murders on the Crumbles. The first, labelled The Séance on the Shingle was a sad little story. Irene Munro, 17, (right) came to Eastbourne for her holidays and on 19 August 1920 she was seen on the Crumbles 'happy and laughing in the company of two men'. Later that day her body was found battered to death. Descriptions of the men were obtained and Jack Field, 19, and William Gray, 28, both unemployed, were apprehended on the seafront. There was little doubt of their guilt, each claimed the other had struck the fatal blow, and both were executed the next year.

To provide work for the unemployed, in 1921-3 the Council erected a wooden tea chalet and shelter on the promenade below the Holywell Italian Gardens at a cost of £912. A brick-built café later replaced the chalet. Local unemployed were also used to lay out gardens at the Redoubt, Gildredge Hospital, the Archery and Gilbert Recreation grounds.

The EAC was one of the firms that failed. Eastbourne Corporation bought buildings in 1924 as a winter store for deck chairs, and the large steel hanger, bought by Wenham's as a furniture repository, lasted until the 1987 'hurricane'.

On the other hand, the Post Office, which had taken over the National Telephone Co in 1911, was expanding, and in 1923 the local exchange transferred to the HPO in Upperton Road. Douglas Swift, a messenger boy, said 'The Post Office was run on military lines, the postmen saluted Major Headley, the Postmaster, who inspected every one before they went on their rounds.'

LAWN TENNIS COURTS & PAVILION
REDOUBT EASTBOURNE.   JUDGES

By the 1920s land to the west of the Redoubt had been laid out as a music garden, around a bandstand. To the east, stretching to Princes Park were bowling greens, an 18-hole putting green, and tennis courts. In 1968 the bandstand was replaced by a sun lounge; since 1994 the Pavilion Tea Rooms.

In 1919 John Chisholm Towner, an Eastbourne auctioneer, estate agent, and Council member, had left a bequest of £6000 and his collection of pictures to the County Borough to form an art gallery. Two years later the Borough paid £19 000 for the Manor House and grounds in Borough Lane, vacated by the Davies Gilbert family. The Towner Art Gallery and Manor Gardens opened in 1923, with Arthur F Reeve-Fowkes, Director of Art at the Technical Institute, as the Curator.

In 1923 Capt. Amers inaugurated an Annual Musical Festival. Some performances were broadcast, and Eric Coates and Sir Edward Elgar, the composer of the *Enigma Variations,* were among the favourite conductors. Eastbourne didn't escape the Jazz Age when dancing was all the rage. Every large store had a thé dansant, and the Winter Garden with Jenkie's Band was another popular venue.

Pupils at Aldro prep. School, now part of the Brighton University Meads campus, included Kim Philby, the double spy, who was head boy in 1924.

That year the Redoubt was finally sold to the Corporation by the Army Council for £150, and opened to the public. The land adjoining the Redoubt had been offloaded by the Duke in 1905.

By now bathing was popular along the whole of the front and at Birling Gap. Sea bathing at Eastbourne is particularly safe with the gentle slope of the foreshore, although at high tide the sloping shingle beaches mean that bathers can be out of their depth just a few steps out.

In the 1920s there were three types of bather: those who used a Corporation bathing cabin to undress and store their clothes (at 2½p for 30 minutes); those who changed in the canvas enclosures, separate for men and women, at each end of the promenade (½p a time), and the quite outrageous 'Mackintosh bathers'. These individuals – already in swim suits covered by a mac - ran to the beach from their house or hotel, swam, and rushed back in a wet costume. Scandalous behaviour.

The Crumbles maintained its popularity for murders, and Sir Bernard Spilsbury, the renowned forensic pathologist, declared that the second Crumbles murder, of Emily Kaye in 1924, was his most interesting case.

Otherwise Eastbourne maintained its pre-eminence as a peaceful holiday town. Hampden Park now had a well-matured look, and was kept in a good state surrounded by a high fence and locked gates at night. One change was in 1926 when Alice Hudson became Eastbourne's first woman Mayor.

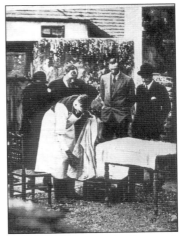

Patrick Mahon, 34, was a persistent philanderer with a record of embezzlement and violent robbery, yet in 1924, Emily Kaye, 37, struck up a relationship though she knew he was married. She found herself pregnant, and told her friends she was going away with 'Pat'. Scotland Yard, having been tipped off, arrested Mahon and he admitted that he went to Eastbourne with Emily. In a rented ex- coastguard cottage the police found a trunk, with initials EBK, which held human body parts. Dr (later Sir) Bernard Spilsbury reassembled them, showing that they were of a pregnant woman. At his trial Mahon convicted himself, and he was hanged at Wandsworth. Dr Spilsbury is seen here conducting part of the post mortem in the garden of the coastguard cottage on the Crumbles.

In 1924 the Duke put Devonshire Park on the market and at last the Borough acquired the Devonshire Baths and Manager's House for £16 500. The Council spent another £17 500 adding Turkish Baths and updating the heating, lavatories and the filtration plant. You can see why the Duke was keen to extricate himself, but the expenditure was worthwhile for the baths were heavily used in the 1930s when mixed bathing came in.

The first Marks and Sparks shop in Eastbourne opened on 27 July 1912 at 51 Terminus Road. It extended to include number 53 in 1937, but was flattened in the terrible 'Christmas bombing' of 1942 when over 50 women and children were killed or injured. After temporary premises it was rebuilt at the old site (now 133/137 Terminus Road) and opened in May 1955.

Eastbourne copied every other town between the wars with long queues as the norm every Friday and Saturday night for admission to its cinemas. There was the *Classic* (Trinity Place, now flats); *Elysium* (a flea pit) and after a refit the *Gaiety*; the *Luxor* Pevensey Road, opened 1933 (later *ABC*); *Mansells New Central* (became the *Manhattan,* closing 1966); some came and went such as the News Theatre in Trinity Place, and they all changed names frequently - *Old Town Cinema / Regent /*

*Plaza.* 'We paid 4d at the *Picturedrome* in Langney Road [later the *Curzon*], black and white and silent, except for the pianist. We fell about over Charlie Chaplin, and Harold Lloyd, but the cowboy films were our favourites.'

The mad frenzy of 'The Pictures' spawned Astaire Avenue, named after Adele Astaire, the film star dancer's sister, who in 1932 married Lord Charles Cavendish.

In the 1920s a battle was being waged against speculative building on the Downs. In their most statesmanlike action Eastbourne Council decided to purchase 4100 acres on Beachy Head, to keep it as open space in perpetuity for all to enjoy. It was finally bought in 1929 for £91291, at £22 per acre. The Duke and Duchess of York opened the commemorative seat.

It wasn't long before shops selling musical instruments began to suffer. S Hermitage & Sons' music emporium was in Terminus Road until the war, and Lindridges, its grand pianos and musical instruments set off with palm trees and the busts of composers, lasted only a few years afterwards; it's now Superdrug.

Eastbourne's Conference Trade started in March 1928 when the YMCA Annual Conference was held in the town. The conference trade was to extend the tourist season and even supplant some of the holiday trade, and Rotary International, who first came in October 1931, continues to choose Eastbourne.

The late 1920s saw the *Grand Hotel* doing well. It had its own farm, its visitors' book was like a world-wide Debrett, and from 1924 to 1939, and for sometime after 1945, it provided the BBC with its earliest long-running success, the Palm Court Orchestra which charmed the listeners. The orchestra included 'the man with the singing violin', Albert Sandler, leader 1924-28. The broadcasts were economical for the BBC: 'a microphone was suspended from a delicate chandelier and the sound was perfect'.

Sporting Eastbourne had national players too. In bowls Clara Johns was not only a national champion, but women's bowling became firmly established on a national scale thanks to her. Cyril Tolley, the British Amateur Golf Champion in 1920 and 1929, lived locally as a child, and later he served as an Eastbourne councillor 1958-62.

With the abolition of the Guardians of the Poor in 1930, the ex-workhouse in Old Town was renamed St Mary's Hospital.

Banks were renowned for paying over the odds for a prime site, and in 1930 the National Provincial bank [now NatWest/Bank of Scotland] bought the *Royal Hotel* (formerly *Railway Hotel* and *Kinburn House*) to build their prestigious Terminus Road branch. The new bank was given decorative ceilings by CG Garrard, while the Star Brewery used the bank's £30 000 to build both the *Prince Albert* in Old Town and the *Horse and Groom* at Polegate, two rewarding ventures.

Caffyn's 1930s Seaside workshop premises. In 1929 Caffyn's sold 1000 cars in a year for the first time. Their publicity booklet of the 1930s stated firmly, 'Caffyn's will only act as agents for British cars – they are not prepared to stock or push the sale of foreign cars'. This total involvement with British marques lasted until 1977 when the company acquired Fiat and Mercedes franchises.

Wealthy residents continued to cruise each winter, keeping on a butler, housekeeper, cook, maids and gardeners at home. Poverty existed in the town, but not on the scale of elsewhere, and when a collection was made for the unemployed, clothing and £1000 was sent to South Wales. The families of local unemployed were also assisted, £1530 being distributed to over 120 persons.

Eastbourne had started to asphalt its streets in 1911, and by the 1930s the water carts that were used to lay the dust on the roads had gone, but you can still see the topping-up hydrants around the town e.g. Gaudick Road, Gildredge Road, St Johns Road, Vicarage Road, Granville Road, Grassington Road, and Seaside (Archery) as shown on the right.

Not that the Eastbourne theatres didn't have attractions, Fay Compton at the Devonshire Park Theatre; Ivor Novello and Cicely Courtneidge at the Pier Theatre, and at the *Royal Hippodrome* you could see Harry Tate and his famous motoring sketch, GH Elliot 'The Chocolate-coloured Coon', and Wilson, Kepple and Betty doing their sand dance. Murray King was in pantomime at the Devonshire Park

Theatre over 1894 to 1935, and famous for his 'transformation scenes'. With no TV, some of the acts toured the country doing the same turn for years.

At Christmas time the big stores, Beale's (now the Co-op), Dale & Kerley (TJ Hughes), Bobby's (Debenhams), and Plummer Roddis (C&H Fabrics) vied to provide the most fantastic Father Christmas arrival and Grotto.

The original pier entrance kiosks from the 1870s were replaced by this set of larger ones in 1912, and they lasted until 1951. The central music pavilion was built in 1924/5. Until 1926 no kiosks opened on a Sunday.

To return to the real world, at the end of 1931 Eastbourne Corporation discovered possible acts of bribery in respect of electrical contracts, and in April 1933 Pirelli Ltd, a local councillor, and a council official, pleaded guilty to various charges and were heavily fined.

For spiritual sustenance the Salvation Army opened another Citadel at Central Avenue, in July 1932, and in 1935 built a hall in Royal Sussex Crescent.

Being Eastbourne's MP in the 1930s appears a chancy line. Edward Marjoribanks, Conservative Unionist MP shot himself in 1932; and his successor, Conservative MP John Slater, died of a heart attack at a public banquet on 15 February 1935. Charles Taylor (later knighted) showed that it wasn't the town's fault; elected unopposed he lasted until 1974, for some overstaying his welcome.

Amy Johnson, the popular aviatrix of the day, landed at Kings Drive in 1930, on what is now the Park College site. The Prince of Wales, later Duke of Windsor, also flew in on 30 June 1931. He came to unveil a tablet commemorating the purchase of Devonshire Park including the Floral Hall, Indian Pavilion, and skating rink for £30 000; lay a foundation stone for an extension to the Princess Alice Hospital; and open Princes Park, formerly the Gilbert Recreation Ground.

The year Hitler became Chancellor of Germany, 1933, was the Golden Jubilee of the Incorporation of the Borough of Eastbourne. It was marked by a week of events, that included an Air Rally, a Carnival, parades, Church Services, a school pageant, a tea for the town's infants (the commemorative mug was presented later because of atrocious weather), and 250 old people went to the *Picturedrome*.

The Diplock Brewery story wasn't finished for Caleb Diplock 'junior', died in 1936 at the age of 95, unmarried without issue, and leaving £527 936. He left his money to 'benevolent and charitable' institutions, and most went to hospitals selected by his executors. In 1940 the will was challenged and eventually the House of Lords determined that the charities had to return any monies received, while 48 distant relatives benefited. The will wasn't cleared up until 1950.

Sir James Purves Stewart, a famous neurologist, who had lived in Eastbourne as a child, bought the Belle Tout lighthouse in 1923 for £1500. He did it up, and entertained King George V and Queen Mary to the views in March 1935.

Their Silver Jubilee in May that year was commemorated along the lines of the 1933 celebrations. A Church Service, day off for Corporation employees - with pay, children and old folk taken to the cinema, fireworks, Morris dancing, floodlighting and a Beachy Head beacon, all for £851.

The 'new' bandstand, built at a cost of £29 000, was opened by Lord Leconfield on 5 August 1935. The same day he opened Helen Garden with its bowling and putting greens. Mrs Helen Hornby Lewis, a 'quiet millionairess' of South Cliff, left the land 'for the perpetual use and enjoyment of the public'. She had also contributed to the Appeal to save Crowlink from development.

The round booking hall was added to Eastbourne station, shops were inserted into the Terminus Road façade and, on 7 July 1935, the first electric train drew in.

Lady Seymour Hicks, daughter of William Terriss, was at the opening of the Terriss Memorial lifeboat museum on 22 March 1937, the first in the UK.

The main event of the year was the Coronation of King George VI and Queen Elizabeth on 10 May 1937. School children gave performances of a *Coronation Cavalcade;* there were dances at the Town Hall and a Ball at the Winter Garden. Territorial Units fired a *feu de joie* at Gildredge Park; the Town Hall had a Grand

Historical Procession, and there was a fireworks display, when many were 'lit up'.

In 1937 the Bill for the extension of Eastbourne received Royal assent, bringing part of Willingdon and much of Langney into the town.

In other ways Eastbourne had changed little, except that Seaside Road from Memorial Square to Terminus Road was transformed into Trinity Trees. Schools and churches still flourished, although most have now gone. A few bathchairs plied for hire on the front, 'The Major' rode his piebald horse up and down from the *Grand Hotel* to the pier, and the tarred surface of Victoria Drive stopped at Downs Avenue. There was a family atmosphere in the town. 'You always met someone you knew in Terminus Road.'

The mild hedonism of the 1920s had subsided, and while businesses had gone to the wall in the early 1930s, the end of the decade saw Eastbourne's bands, deck chairs, and sea bathing produce a surplus of £8000, easily covering a small loss on the Devonshire Baths - and the buses made a profit too.

The day of the local fishermen, shown here spratting, was ending. The Hide family connection finished in the 1930s; by 2000 not one of the old families was in fishing.

Eastbourne hadn't fared too badly. The Edwardian summer had been followed by some autumnal winds of change, but hardly a fall. The Snoot Parade and most steam locomotives had gone, as had adverts for maids in Meads at £52 a year. The Royal Ladies Golf Club had closed, for now women were admitted to the Royal. In 1938 the economy and the world situation seemed to be bucking up, and Jeffery Farnol, author of over 40 books, moved into 14 Denton Road where he lived until his death in 1952. The Council, like others, sent a message of congratulations to Neville Chamberlain for his 'Peace in our Time' trip to Munich.

The next year, after the Nazi takeover of Czechoslovakia, the Munich euphoria was fading. The heartfelt wish was for a magical Pantomime Transformation, but what appeared over Eastbourne in January 1939 was the Aurora Borealis. People said the flickering curtains and lurid colours in the sky presaged a disaster.

# 5. From Safe Zone to the Front Line, 1939-45

"Mummy, why are those ladies deformed?" asked the little girl, indicating a group of pregnant women. "Don't point Margaret dear; they're London evacuees pretending to be anti-aircraft barrage balloons".

Such was Eastbourne's approach to the practicalities of the Second World War, and no doubt to sex as well. The town was well ahead with its national war preparations; over 60 000 gas masks had been distributed, and its first air-raid siren trials (albeit steam-driven) had been held on 28 July 1938, but Eastbournians assumed any war to be much the same as 1914-18. Hadn't Eastbourne's MP, Charles Taylor, expressed it clearly enough in the spring of 1939? "Attackers would not go to the trouble of carrying high-explosive bombs for Eastbourne."

A Supermarine Stranraer seaplane landed near to Eastbourne pier just before the war as part of a recruiting drive. It clearly produced a response from interested local rowers. Major T Henry Wilson of the local TA went round giving talks at cinemas to encourage recruits.

Air Raid Precautions, ARP, were taken seriously, for raids with poison gas were expected as soon as war was declared, but as anticipated the town was designated a Safe Zone and warned to receive evacuees from London if war came.

The messy horrors of war, however, came early to the town. On August Bank Holiday, 1939, an RAF Blenheim bomber on exercises crashed into the Beachy Head cliff in heavy mist, killing the crew of three - and a young woman who just happened to be walking there.

As part of the million school children moved from towns and cities to the safety of the countryside, trainloads of evacuees started arriving at Eastbourne on Friday, 1 September, and poured in over three days. Little Londoners, with their name-labels and gas masks, those pregnant mums, and the infirm, were all moved on by bus, car and ambulance to billets in private homes or hospitals.

Some businesses evacuated themselves. The National Amalgamated Approved Society's staff came from London to the empty Temple Grove School buildings.

Altogether almost 20 000 descended on the town, adding another third to its population. The local authority under the Town Clerk, Francis Busby, one of those wonderful municipal officials who ran the place, had everything under control.

Eastbourne's war, like the rest of the country, started with the 'phoney war' from September 1939 to the early summer of 1940.

The black-out was unpopular. Night time was pitch dark, and road traffic accidents soared, but "Put that Light Out" became the catch phrase, and as early as 20 September a Willingdon resident was fined £10 for showing a light. The snowy 1939-40 winter was not helped by an unpatriotic epidemic of German measles.

Eastbourne's first taste of action and bravery came on 20 March 1940 off Beachy Head. A German plane bombed the 5430-ton *ss Barnhill,* which drifted on fire and ran aground near Langney Point. The lifeboat took off the survivors, but later the weird sound of the ship's bell was heard, so the lifeboat put out again and two lifeboatmen scrambled onto the stricken ship, to discover that the captain, blown off the bridge and assumed missing, had managed to crawl back and grip the bell rope with his teeth, in spite of extensive injuries. His rescuers, Alec Huggett and Tom Allchorn, were awarded RNLI Bronze Medals.

Even so, it seemed that war, as ever, would be profitable for Eastbourne. Cecil Page, the chairman, told *Grand Hotel* shareholders at the AGM in 1940 that up to May 1940 business had been excellent.

The first phase of air-raids, from 3 July 1940 to 7 June 1941, opened for real on the morning of Sunday, 7 July, when a single, low-flying Dornier Do17 dropped a stick of high-explosive [HE] bombs along Whitley Road from St Philip's Avenue to Avondale Road. Two people died. The house has criss-cross anti-splinter tape on the windows.

That all altered when the Germans overran the Netherlands, Belgium and France. Eastbourne's small craft helped in the May-June 1940 Dunkirk evacuation, where two local pleasure boats and a fishing boat were sunk. The town's *Jane Holland* lifeboat truly demonstrated the Bulldog Spirit. Hit by over 500 missiles, rammed, and finally abandoned, two days afterwards the lifeboat was found floating in the Channel by the Royal Navy and towed to Dover where she was repaired and returned to Eastbourne to serve for another nine years.

Overnight Eastbourne went from Safety Zone to the Front Line. You were prohibited from entering a coastal belt south of Polegate unless a resident or you had business there. Mothers-about-to-be were packed up country to East Grinstead.

The beach was dotted with poles, spikes and wire to stop planes landing, and mined. All civilians were told to keep a case packed so that they could leave immediately if they heard the ringing of the church bells, the invasion signal.

The Army came to blow up the pier while Clarkson Rose's End-of-the-Pier Show *Twinkle* was running. They were persuaded to wait until the end of the performance, by which time it was decided not to destroy it, but to confuse the Germans by removing planks and installing guns on the theatre and at the entrance.

On 21 July 1940 over 3000 Eastbourne children were sent to the Home Counties. Very sensible too, for Eastbourne had no defences or much in the way of shelters. Over the subsequent months, as the Battle of Britain raged overhead, Eastbourne had at least one raid almost every day.

On 16 August 1940 the lattice work of vapour trails, the roaring of engines, the rattling of guns above, and the crump of bombs below, were heightened as a Messerschmitt Me 110 screamed out of the sky to dive into the grounds of the Aldro School at Meads. This raid stimulated the town to hit back and the *Eastbourne Gazette and Herald* sponsored a Spitfire Fund. A Spitfire cost £5000, then the price of ten houses, and within a week Eastbourne had raised £6000.

These early attacks generated indignation for it was felt that Eastbourne was not a legitimate target. This mood changed as troops were stationed in the town, the Downs were used for training, radar equipment blossomed on Beachy Head, fighting vehicles were tested for amphibious use, and the area was used as a staging post for raids into France.

Left: the *Lion Inn* before and below after the bombing of Sunday, 10 November 1940.

The licensee, Charles Rich, stayed in bed and was killed, his wife who went into the cellar, survived.

A proclamation of 10 September encouraged people to leave, the population fell from 60 000 to around 10 000, and grass grew in the centre of town roads.

The railway station was crowded on Friday, 13 September with people being evacuated when the town was raided by at least five planes. Bombs were dropped on Seaside and the town centre, where in both Hyde Road and Gildredge Road solicitors' offices were destroyed and legal papers were found 750m away in Pevensey Road. Two 250kg bombs fell on the Seaside recreation ground, one failing to explode, to be mentioned later.

The next day began on a high note when two Spitfires attacked a Dornier bomber over the town and sent it into the sea, but otherwise it was a day of noise, dust and debris. In four raids German aircraft dropped HE and incendiary bombs from the *Burlington Hotel* on the front to Old Town, and from Lottbridge Drove on the east to Meads in the west, and later Dorniers attacked the Beachy Head radar.

Saturday, 28 September, witnessed scenes of exceptional gallantry and courage. Four bombs hit Tideswell Road, Bourne Street, and Cavendish Place, where eight persons were trapped in cellars. Surgeon Lawrence Snowball said, "Five were rescued, but a 17-year-old Hankham girl - I still recall her name, Miss Peggy Harland - was pinned by a steel girder across her ankles." She was in great pain, and unable to move, yet she kept up her spirits and those of her rescuers, toiling despite a nearby unexploded bomb [UXB] and the need for constant pumping of leaking water. "After 24 hours when it was apparent that she could not be released, Dr Roy Barron and myself crawled to her: he to give the anaesthetic and me to amputate both legs. Sadly, Miss Harland died in hospital two days later." She was posthumously awarded the Girl Guides' Gilt Cross, and 14 gallantry awards were made to the rescuers.

The detonator being removed from an unexploded bomb - with care. Some bombs didn't go off because they hadn't been primed, others were faulty, and some were delayed action – timed to go off 2-3 hours after the raid to hamper rescue work. The sergeant of a local Bomb Disposal Squad and a policeman died when a UXB went off near the present Ashford Road car park.

Harry Homewood, of the rescue services, described his experience when Pickford's upholstery store was bombed, and a raft of concrete had to be jacked up before a man could be released. "I crawled in and found his legs had been crushed, however, my main hindrances were the tin-tacks. I splinted his legs, but when I tried to ease my way out with him I found my route blocked by another rescuer. He was so petrified with fear that the jacks would collapse on him that he was unable to move. We finally conveyed the injured man to hospital where he recovered."

There were some close shaves as well. On 10 October a high-flying Junkers Ju88 scored a direct hit on St Mary's Church, Decoy Drive. It demolished the building apart from the bell tower, but there were no casualties - when a short time before the church had been fully in use as a communal dining centre.

About this time there was so much damage around Bourne Street that it was known as 'Bomb Alley', or 'Hell Fire Corner'. Venn Claydon said, "If you were brave enough to walk along Terminus Road, it was not exceptional to go all the way from the station to Bolton Road without seeing a single passer-by."

Despite much damage the casualties were few, due almost certainly to the evacuation of the town, in contrast to the loss of life in the Coventry raid. The locals maintained their sense of humour. After one raid a survivor called at the *Cavendish* Saloon Bar for stiff refreshment, but as he put it, 'At the door I saw that a UXB had beaten me to it, but had not yet attracted the barman's attention'.

Many buildings were commandeered. What is now Upperton United Reformed Church housed bombed-out families; All Saints' Hospital was used for troops once again; *Acacia Villa* clinic in Wartling Road became a Civil Defence First Aid station. The old Smallpox Hospital, just east of today's Sovereign harbour, and not in use since an outbreak in 1929, was a guard post; it was demolished in 1946.

Empty schools and hotels were taken over by the armed forces. The *Rustington Court Hotel* was a WRNS billet, the *Lansdowne* the Home Guard HQ, and Roborough School in Upper Avenue had Canadians. The WAAF occupied the *Mostyn Hotel* until it was bombed in March 1943; the site is now *Grand Court.* The Royal Navy had Eastbourne College, Granville House School, and Ranny's School of Domestic Economy, and throughout the war she and a small staff cooked for the sailors of 'HMS Ranny'. What a happy ship!

Perhaps there had not been an invasion – yet, but Eastbourne's raids continued, the majority by bombers abandoning a raid on London.

In April 1941, the future 11th Duke and Duchess of Devonshire spent their two-week honeymoon in Eastbourne. Lord Andrew Cavendish, as he was, on leave from the Coldstream Guards, recalled, "We heard the bombers flying overhead at night. It was an eerie sound which we will never forget". The Duchess is reputed to say that it put her off Eastbourne.

Mans' best friend wasn't forgotten in the war. Here a dog is being rescued from his master's bombed home. RSPCA Inspector Teddie Winn often placed himself at risk to save an animal.

John Claremont writes, 'In February 1942 I arrived in the town as an RAF aircrew cadet for a course on navigation in the *Cavendish Hotel.* The first time I did the calculation Eastbourne had moved to Hertfordshire'.

On 4 May 1942 the east wing of the *Cavendish* was blasted almost into Herts, when Eastbourne's next phase of air raids started, the terrifying 'Hit-and-Run' attacks. Nine bomb-carrying Me 109 fighters flew low across the Channel to avoid the radar, lifted to clear Beachy Head, and swept over the town. The bombs struck the railway line, the station, St John's Church, and a gas holder. On the run home the planes fired at a fishing boat in the bay, badly wounding fishermen Alec Huggett and Micky Andrews. What incensed the locals was that William Joyce, Lord Haw-Haw, broadcasting that night on 'Jarmany Calling', described their boat as an armed trawler. A slight exaggeration, but then rumours were an essential part of wartime life, from 'The Germans have landed' to 'There are oranges at the greengrocers'. It wasn't fantasy, however, to say that the radar units on Beachy Head could view German TV from Paris.

On 13 May 1942 King George VI visited his Armoured Division on the Eastbourne Downs, although the town only learnt of it later.

News was received of the loss at sea of Eric Ravilious, an Eastbourne artist, famed for his distinctive work and for picturing submarine life in the war.

Above, Barclays Bank before, and right, just after the bombing of 7 March 1943. Below before reopening in 1958. Lower right, the new bank inside had no security screens and no 'financial consultants'.

By now petrol rationing was severe and most people left their car in the garage jacked up on bricks 'for the duration'. A strictly observed regulation in coastal towns was that if you left the car you had to immobilise it by removing the rotor arm. With the Battle of the Atlantic not going well, everyone was encouraged to grow more food – Dig for Victory. Every plot became a vegetable patch: Gildredge Park was dug over, and the Carpet Gardens grew onions. The Downs were ploughed almost up to the cliff edge in the drive to produce more food, but even hay-making had its risks, Derrick Pyle recalls diving for cover, "There was low cloud, the threshing machine was whirling away, and the first we noticed was when we saw spurts of earth across the field as the planes fired their cannon shells."

Derek Keay was walking by Motcombe baths in Old Town when a Focke-Wulf

FW190 swept over with guns firing. "My wife and I dived in somewhere, but we could hear the bullets hitting the roof of the shelter. Another time we were near the main Post Office in Upperton Road when six Me 109s strafed Terminus Road and Upperton, it was most frightening."

Arthur Edward Rush, Eastbourne's Mayor at the outbreak of war, was an independent councillor and he was re-elected in November 1939, and again 1940-2. He worked in a quiet, unassuming manner, consoling bombed-out victims and getting things done, and he was a leader in the campaign for a local air-raid warning for the town.

There had been no warning of the first raid on Eastbourne in July 1940, and by the autumn air-raid warnings were a joke; as one victim put it, "Just as I arrived at the hospital the air-raid siren sounded the alarm". Stanley Apps remembers waiting for a bus in Eldon Road, "There was no siren, and suddenly three planes came round the Beehive Plantation and started firing at Old Town".

After the error alert at the beginning of the war, caused by a single French aircraft, sirens were not sounded for single aircraft, which didn't help Eastbourne. The air-raid warning area controller was 30 miles away and hence Eastbourne endured unheralded bombing. It was too easy for German planes to sweep in low from the sea, and dash away before any authorised alarm. At last, representations by the Town Council and the local press led to a local siren that gave about half-a-minute's warning, enough to dash for cover. This separate 'Cuckoo' warning, so-called after the noise it made, was first heard on 6 June 1942.

About a week subsequent to the Dieppe Raid, German planes dropped bundles of propaganda leaflets over the town. They showed captured Allied troops and their burnt-out equipment, but nobody took too much notice of them except for the audience in one of the cinemas, where a bundle failed to unwrap during its descent and crashed through the cinema roof.

Eastbourne's heaviest night raid on 11 August 1942 saw flares from waves of bombers light up the town, and widespread damage by HE and incendiary bombs in Seaside, Meads, Babylon Down, Grove Road, The Avenue, the railway station, Terminus Road and Willingdon, and St Anne's Church was burnt out.

This was a week before *Operation Jubilee,* the ill-fated, but informative Dieppe raid of 19 August, and many residents thought that the Germans had got wind of the attack, with the Canadians practising tank battles and artillery firing on the Downs, and Newhaven was a departure port for the raid. *Chaseley*, in South Cliff, was also the 1st Canadian Special Wireless Section's communications control centre during the raid, and part of the fighter cover took off from Friston airfield, two of these planes being lost, so Eastbourne was a fair enough target.

FW190 fighter-bombers struck again and again. On 13 August 1942 they crossed the coast at Cooden and came in from the east, and on 16 September they had another go at the station, killing six railwaymen. These raids confirmed that the fighter-bombers, such as Me 109s, carrying medium-capacity 250kg bombs, were more accurate than high-level bombers, and that the FW 190, which could carry a 1000kg bomb load, had become a menace; so much so that a Spitfire squadron was later installed at Friston airfield.

The hospitals were kept busy, it was not uncommon to treat 50 casualties at a time, working with windows blown in.

Barbara Picard wrote in her diary, 'Sunday 7/3/43. While we were having lunch the Germans made their usual Sunday raid and dropped bombs on Jevington Gardens, Cornfield Road, Panto's sweet factory and Barclays Bank.'

Locals thought that the Germans switched off their engines as they glided in, and restarted them to make their escape. It wasn't possible, however, for them to re-start their engines in flight, they merely boosted the engine for the getaway.

Terminus Road after a 500kg bomb in the raid of 3 April 1943. A gas main is on fire, people were trapped in a cellar on the left, and Dale & Kerley's store opposite (now TJ Hughes) took some of the impact. This was the raid when a Spencer Road shelter was hit with great loss of life, and the Park Gates Hotel was also wrecked.

Stanley Apps' opinion was that, "In the Hit-and-Run raids you didn't have time to get to a shelter, you just dived under a table. It wasn't a normal life, but it became so". A few Morrison indoor table shelters were issued, but not enough, so the Borough Surveyor enterprisingly produced a wooden-framed replica. This was ridiculed until both types were tested by dropping a load of bricks on them, when the local 'Morrison' stood up to the weight better than the metal-framed one.

Mrs Ruth Tucker has memories of the bombing of 4 June 1943 when the Technical Institute and shops were hit. "I went out to find that scattered all along The

Avenue were books from the Library and fish from MacFisheries. People were picking up food for both mind and body."

Don't think that people didn't enjoy themselves. Gordon Rider's band played nightly at the Winter Garden and with so many troops training on the Downs there was no shortage of partners for the local women. Golfers were able to fit in a round too, although there were extra hazards with upright poles driven into the fairways to catch invading gliders - and deflect the occasional golf ball.

One popular recreation that assisted the war effort was to help with the harvest. Farmer Lewis Pyle of Chalk Farm welcomed family parties. "As we played our small part to bring the harvest safely home, high overhead, scarcely audible, our bombers were setting out. We did not have to be reminded that many would not be coming back." Many damaged planes from both sides crashed into the sea and Downland around the town.

It is possible that Eastbourne received the first casualties from the Normandy landings. Early on 6 June 1944 an aircraft carrying paratroopers over France was peppered when an anti-aircraft shell burst underneath. Ordered to return, it just managed to bellyflop at Friston airfield. Mr Snowball, a surgeon, said, "At the hospital we spent the rest of the night digging out bits of shrapnel from them".

Charleston Road after a Flying Bomb (V1). The first flying bomb, or PAC (Pilotless Aircraft) or Doodlebug, was seen from Beachy Head, on the night of 12-13 June, heading for London where almost all were targeted; Eastbourne and the south coast only received malfunctioning or misdirected ones. Merely 15 landed in the Borough; although much damage resulted to property, and many civilians were injured, none died.

The first of Hitler's Victory or Vengeance weapons, hence V1s, came next. Over the next two months there was an incident every few days, and Eastbourne residents learnt to listen out for the sound of the engine. If it kept going the Doodlebug was passing over towards some other unfortunate, if it cut out, you got down, for there would be an explosion within a few seconds: a worrying time.

Lawrence Snowball commented, "It was thanks to the bravery of all the D-Day troops that Eastbourne was saved from prolonged V1 bombardment. One of the most remarkable features of everyday life was the wonderful spirit. If a family was bombed-out they would receive offers of accommodation, clothes and food, often from people quite unknown to them". Some of the restrictions were, however, being eased and the ending of the black-out was an especially joyful moment.

In October 1944, perhaps as the start of reconciliation, the Rt Revd George Bell, Bishop of Chichester, dedicated the murals of German-born artist, Hans Feibusch, in war-damaged St Elisabeth's Church.

There was discussion about whether Glenn Miller, the American band leader, had died off Beachy Head on 15 December 1944. He was in a Norseman flying to Paris when 138 Lancaster bombers returning from an aborted raid jettisoned their bombs into the Channel and reported that an explosion was seen below.

At the outbreak of war Eastbourne had awaited some 20 000 evacuees with trepidation. In February 1945 the town greeted unreservedly the 10 000 repatriated Australian prisoners-of-war who were billeted around the town, or in some instances admitted to St Mary's Hospital, while they waited to board their ships for home. Mrs Florence Tomsett and Mrs Doris Pumfrey were Red Cross members who lent a hand, "We visited some of the lads in hospital, taking toiletries to them and writing letters if they weren't well enough themselves." The Aussies helped to renovate the Saffrons' county cricket pitch from five years of neglect and at least one bomb on the square. After helping to celebrate VE Day, and a Grand Thank You Garden Party for the town on 6 July 1945, they were soon on their way.

In another twist of fate, Black Friday, 13 September 1940, came back to haunt the town. The UXB that had fallen on the Seaside Recreation ground that day had penetrated so deeply that it had been left. The spot was marked and by custom the bomb was given a nickname. On 3 January 1946, 'Hermann' was dug out from 7m down, with the BBC broadcasting the big bang. The last bomb site wasn't built over until the 1980s, and in 2001 an estate agent estimated that 10% of Eastbourne's buildings had evidence of war damage. Not surprising, for against all the predictions Eastbourne was the most often bombed town on the south coast.

A resident who went through the war in Eastbourne said, "I have no hatred for Germans, but they deserved all they got. One hope that kept us going in 1940 was that eventually they would be given what they threw at us, if not more."

Eastbourne's heroism was perpetuated in more appropriate ways. *Thornton Court,* in Bourne Street, built on the site of 139 'Bomb Alley' damaged properties, has a wall plaque unveiled in 1952 which reads, '…erected by Eastbourne Corporation as a tribute to the fortitude shown by the inhabitants of the town during the air raids of the war of 1939-45…'

# 6. Update on an Ever-Changing Town

Post-war Eastbourne needed to recover its position as a leading holiday resort, but while every holiday town needed some tarting-up, Eastbourne had to cope with 500 buildings destroyed, twice that rendered uninhabitable, and 5000 damaged.

Work started clearing the seafront of invasion defences and mines, and among the measures to ease the housing shortage, over 200 'pre-fabs' were erected – glorified huts of aluminium and asbestos cement – with German prisoners-of-war digging out the foundations.

A public meeting decided that Eastbourne's War Memorial should include houses for the war disabled. The Duke of Devonshire donated the land in Victoria Drive. Twelve houses were the aim but, because of some dissention and insufficient funds, only six houses were opened in 1952 at a cost of £17405. The architect, FC Benz, gave his services gratis. Many improvements and additions have been made over the years.

Francis Busby led the recovery and the new Entertainments Manager, George Hill, provided the energy and hard work to promote the town as a top resort.

The *Grand Hotel,* used by the RAF during the war, discarded its roof-mounted anti-aircraft gun and reopened in September 1946. It has had many additions and improvements over the years and remains Eastbourne's top 5-star hotel.

The old Belle Tout lighthouse was a 'friendly-fire' war ruin (shown left in the 1930s and right in 1945). Sir James Purves Stewart gifted it to the Council after pocketing £5000 war compensation. Dr ER Cullinan leased it in 1955, and had made it sound by 1960. Since restored and moved.

The pier also reopened in 1946 in spite of severe damage from enemy fire and a mine exploding near the beach. The music pavilion was converted to a ballroom and the theatre starred the Summer Show, with Sandy Powell's Starlight and his catch phrase 'Can you hear me mother' running most years between 1948 and 1970. The entrance kiosks of 1912 were replaced in 1951.

Only eight private schools returned after the war. Since then the Ascham, Chelmsford Hall and Neville House sites have been developed, and Beresford House School which moved in 1939 from The Avenue to Summerdown Road closed in 1991. The main building was demolished in 1995 and the grounds are now part of Eastbourne College's sports pitches.

A Teachers' Training College for 200 demobbed troops opened at Meads in 1947, and that year the Chelsea College of Physical Education, with 90 students, transferred from London to Eastbourne. Chelsea College prospered and the Queen opened a new building in October 1966, and it is now part of Brighton University.

The bombed out Technical Institute students and four teachers found rooms at *The Grange,* a private school in St Anne's Road dating from 1878 but closed after 1940. The College extended to *St Helena's* school next door and spread around St Anne's Road, and *Eversley Court,* after the boys' school went to Kings Drive. From 1995 the now South Downs College was on the Cross Levels Way site and all departments were moved there by 1997. The old campus was sold for housing.

The late 1940s and 1950s were happy days for the holiday industry. People wanted an escape from the tedium of austerity, yet it was before the Costa package holiday – 5000 watched the band of the Irish Guards play at the Royal Parade Bandstand on Good Friday 1950. All the local businesses did well; the hotels, the shops, all the theatres, and Allchorn's 'Round the Bay' trips.

The Corporation Buses got into the act by slicing the tops off five buses, and painting them white to use as open-top 'Round the Town' buses for the visitors.

In 1948 Lloyds of London donated the Beachy Head Watch Tower to the Council; topless, it is now a viewing platform with a telescope. You can find some of the guy rope supports for the semaphore mast. The signalman's hut, latterly in use as a Countryside Centre, was torched in 1992 and later all trace expunged.

Edward, 10th Duke of Devonshire, enjoyed his visits to Compton Place (right) and delighted in the local forestry, but in November 1950 he died of a heart attack while cutting down a tree. His unexpected death at 55 meant that death duties came to £4.7m, but the new Duke and Duchess tackled the situation with vigour and paid off all the debts within 16 years. The Eastbourne ground rents must have helped; however, they had to sell off some land in Sussex including Abbott's Wood near Arlington.

Another notable, Sir Charles Sherrington, physiologist and Nobel laureate, died at Eastbourne in 1952.

The nip of the Cold War was in the air and between 1950 and 1953 the Coastguard Cottages on Beachy Head were demolished and a substantial underground nuclear war bunker built. In the way of such matters it was declared redundant in 1957 having been superseded by new technology. Until the 1990s you could see the above-ground Guard House, latterly used by the coastguard and police. It was demolished after replacement huts were provided nearer the hotel.

The 1953 Coronation had a dramatic effect on a drab country of rationing, bomb sites, and lack of choice. For many the Royal anointing was their first television program. Locally, the Golden Jubilee of Eastbourne Girls' High School was celebrated that year (left headmistresses C Adams and L Gunnery), but the Prep. School (seen right in 1935) was allowed to run down.

Petrol rationing finished in 1950 and in 1954 new cars became available from stock for the first time since the war, resulting in record profits for dealers.

Building restrictions were also lifted in 1954, and many of Eastbourne's gaps were filled. The Park Gates site was reconstructed in the early 1950s, *Grand Court* and *Metropole Court* replaced bombed hotels and in 1966 a new style east wing of the *Cavendish Hotel* was completed.

Princess Alice, Countess of Athlone, distributed the prizes at the 1953 Princess Alice Hospital Nurses' Prizegiving. She had broken her wrist, but gamely attended and told the story about the rugby player in the Casualty department who was complaining bitterly about having his dislocated shoulder replaced. When one of the nurses snapped that she had heard less noise from a mother who had just given birth, his reply was, "I bet she'd complain enough if you tried to put it back again".

Between 1954 and 1969 Eastbourne had a miniature tramway (right). This 'Crumbles Tramway' ran from Royal Parade past Prince's Park to the Crumbles. Extended in 1959, but moved to Seaton, Devon. The ubiquitous Dotto train started here in 1988. Three trains, Romeo, Juliet and Cupid operate in season along the front from the Sovereign Leisure Centre to Holywell.

Holidays abroad were slow to start after the war, understandably when in 1946 each person was only allowed to take £25 out of the country. The first coach tour from Eastbourne was in 1950, when coaches had to be taken aboard ship by crane, and it was 1952 before the first ramps were built at Dover. When overseas holidays took off in the 1960s the hotels and businesses relied more and more on the conference trade, product launches, and 'Golden Oldies' especially out of season.

To reduce the seasonal unemployment in the town the Council took the first steps towards an Industrial Park when, in 1954, Armour & Co, a subsidiary of an American pharmaceutical company, established a factory of some 30 000 sq. ft with 250 employees, on the Brampton Road Trading Estate. It was a pleasant, clean business, and proved to be the catalyst to stimulate other companies to come to Eastbourne. Now there are many Industrial Estates. The Council took measures to develop the services for them, and Lottbridge Drove opened for traffic in 1964.

Among local residents were George Elrick, singer and big band leader of the 1940s and 50s; and Francis Maurice Brown (1881-1955), playwright, poet, and theatrical impresario, and son of the founder of St Bede's School. Another, until his death in 2003, was theatrical personality, actor Hubert Gregg. In one of his books he describes driving to Beachy Head in the mid-1950s when under stress at work.

On 26 April 1955 the Greek ship *Germania* came ashore in fog at Cow Gap after a collision. The lifeboat landed 23 of the crew, but the captain and other crew stayed on board. On 6 May heavy seas forced the rescue of the men left aboard, a difficult task with the lifeboat almost grounding at times. Coxswain Thomas Allchorn was awarded a bar to his Bronze Medal, presented on 14 March 1956 by the Duchess of Kent, whom he had escorted on a visit to the lighthouse ten years before.

Alfred George Course, a mercantile marine captain, lived in Eastbourne 1957-63. He wrote books about the sea, and his daughter, Pamela Mansbridge, a children's writer, lived at Lullington Close.

Uncle Bertie's Hour was a show of conjuring, ventriloquism, fancy dress parades and talent contests at the Redoubt Music Garden that attracted the morning crowds throughout the summer from 1949 to 1963. Uncle Bertie, Bertram Otto, also built model railways, one of which he exhibited at the Winter Garden with 'nearly a mile of track' and '23 stations'. Those were the days when a local paper could enthuse 'he is unmarried and adores children'.

The post-war restoration continued. St John the Evangelist Church in Meads was rebuilt with help from the War Damage Commission 1955-7. The tower remained of the former church, but required restoration. The ground floor was converted into a chapel in memory of all those who gave their lives for the cause of freedom in the two world wars, and one of the three bells was sold to Wellington Cathedral (NZ) in 1977 as the church authorities decided that the structure was not strong enough to ring them all.

Marks & Spencer had opened a temporary shop in 1943 on the other side of Terminus Road, until in 1955 a replacement store was erected on the old bomb site, where it is today. The new store was to undergo enlargement and a conversion of the first floor offices to shopping space.

The ruins of St Anne's Church in Upperton Gardens were demolished for housing in 1955, but a piece of masonry was used as a foundation stone of St Richard's, Langney in 1957.

Frederick Soddy, Oxford's first Nobel Laureate, died in September 1956. Born 1877 in Bolton Road, he went to Eastbourne College and Merton College graduating with first class honours in Chemistry. A radiochemist, he collaborated with Rutherford and Ramsay, and coined the term 'isotope' for different forms of the same element. He was related to Gilbert Soddy of Gilbert's the Bakers, who was Mayor of Eastbourne 1922-4.

After the war Miss Randall was 60, but more girls wanted catering as a career, so she decided to carry on the School of Domestic Economy, and the school extended from 1 to 11 Silverdale Road with hostels in Jevington Gardens and South Cliff. By now girls could be out till midnight although, on good authority, Eastbourne College boys climbed the drainpipes in the early hours. At the School's Golden Jubilee in 1957 'Ranny' was presented with a mink jacket and a wedding cake, which she said she had always wanted. By now there were 200 students, including mature ones, and catering demonstrations were given. 'Ranny' died in May 1959 and the college closed in 1996.

Traffic lights were installed outside the station in June 1955 replacing the policeman on point duty there directing the traffic, now there's a roundabout as well. Eastbourne's first traffic wardens took up their duties on 1 April 1964.

The Redoubt Model Village, was designed and built by Benjamin White within the walls of the old fort. Most of the models were exact scale replicas of actual buildings and Fountains Abbey, which dominated the site, took nine months to construct. Opened to the public in 1957 it soon became a major attraction. The dry moat, when terraced-over, became another of Ben's ventures when, in 1961, he developed the Blue Temple Grotto and Aquarium.

In 1960 the Redoubt was declared an Ancient Monument, and in 1973 when Peter Bedford was Director of Tourism and Entertainment the Council took over the Model Village and Aquarium, and commenced a £100 000 renovation program under the Curator, David Galer. The Marquis of Abergavenny officially opened the 'new' Redoubt, restored to its original condition, on 18 May 1979, and, in spite of damp, it houses the extensive Sussex Combined Services Museum and is used for exhibitions, concerts and firework displays.

July 1956 to July 1957 could be described as the year of Dr John Bodkin Adams (1899-1983), local general practitioner. Gossip about the 'Eastbourne Bluebeard' spread from the town, around the country, to all over the world. He was accused of the murder of three patients for gain, although the press declared there were 400 victims. In Paul Harris' words, 'The best publicity the town could have had, it was very good for business'.

It was true, the town was prospering. Despite a little hiccup when the Suez crisis of 1956 brought Territorial activity to the Ordnance Yard in Seaside, along with petrol coupons and credit restrictions, Louis G Ford's, the local ironmongers now Graham's, more than doubled their turnover in the 1950s.

Another power in Eastbourne at that time was Sir Roland V Gwynne, DSO DL (1882-1971). 'Roley', of *Folkington Manor,* had been Mayor of Eastbourne 1928-31, Chairman of the Board of Guardians 1928-30, was a Freeman of the Borough, on the Eastbourne and Hailsham benches, and chairman of both 1951-57. Before 1951, when the chairman rotated, he would telephone to determine if he was chairman for the day and if he wasn't he didn't bother to turn up. A terrible driver, and gruff at times, he was a capable and kindly man; on more than one occasion he anonymously paid the rates for an unfortunate arraigned in front of him for arrears.

Ellen Maud Thornton also had the Freedom of the Borough, perhaps because she was said to look like Queen Victoria. On the Council from 1920 to her death in 1962, she was the daughter of a Mayor, and she was Mayor 1934-36. She worked hard for the welfare of the blind and strove for the Blind Centre.

In 1957 Harold Wenham of the Eastbourne Round Table resolved to revive the pre-war Carnival Procession. The Eastbourne Lions Club took it over in 1970 and continued this successful local occasion up to 1998.

Although the Nursing Sisters returned in 1945 to All Saints' Hospital, by 1959 they found that they could no longer continue. Ultimately, the hospital was taken over by the NHS, becoming mainly a rehabilitation hospital for the elderly, with a stroke unit, and after 1996 a day hospital. It closed with some acrimony in 2004.

The idea of building a new conference and concert hall was mooted in 1950. In 1955 the Council contemplated building the Congress Theatre in place of the Wish Tower, and followed this by threatening to knock down the Tower for a café.

More conservation minded, Gilbert Samuel Foyle (1886-1971), a founder of Foyle's Bookshop, was a member of Eastbourne Council 1952-62. His donation in

1957 enabled the Council to buy 94 acres of the Downs near Whitbread Hollow; and Foyle Way was the name given to a path from the western seafront towards Whitbread Hollow. Another good deed in 1961 funded the café and sun lounge close to the Wish Tower. By now the Wish Tower had been listed, renovated, and opened to the public as a museum, and for Myland's puppet shows.

On Monday, 25 August 1958, a steam-hauled train from Glasgow ran into a waiting electric train at Eastbourne station. Five persons were killed instantly, including the driver of the local train. The 23 seriously injured casualties went to the Princess Alice Hospital, one died that day, but the rest made good progress, including a man who used up all the hospital's blood supply, in his blood group, as the surgeons grappled with a ruptured spleen.

Sir Frederick Handley Page (1885-1962), aeronautical engineer, who owned the *Chatsworth Hotel,* died in Eastbourne and is buried in Langney cemetery. Dr Ronald MacQueen also died in 1962. Born in Eastbourne he joined his father, Thomas, in the Bolton Road surgery, the town's oldest. Although called 'Codface' by the nurses, he had an extensive surgical practice. He never learnt to drive a car, and as his chauffeur would not go out in the dark, he used a bicycle on night calls.

The Indian Pavilion (left) at Devonshire Park was demolished in 1961 to make way for the 1600-seat Congress Theatre (right) opened by Princess Margaret in 1963.

The Borough Council bought the *Royal Hippodrome,* Seaside Road, in 1962 to lease out, after leasing it for five years. Formerly the *Theatre Royal,* when built it was one of the first theatres to have a concrete fire escape. In the 1960s and 70s Jack Tripp and Don Smoothey were popular performers there.

Pococks Farm, demolished 1962/3 for development of the Rodmill estate, was believed to be the old 15th century Manor House of Beverington.

Since the bombing the library had been in temporary premises, so the opening of the present Central Library on 6 April 1964 was welcome. The Llewellyn-build is finished in Portland stone and some Lakeland Green slate. The sculpture on the south side represents 'A Scholar Seeking Knowledge' by Hammond Davis.

The local telephone exchange in the HPO, Upperton Road, had 300 staff until June 1966 when the town was converted to automatic working. In 1971 a cordless switchroom opened at Selwyn Road and the HPO room closed.

Bondolfi's in Cornfield Terrace was the place for a cake and a chat. Director Alex Bransgrove says, "We processed 1¼ ton of chocolate a month".

The tale of Eastbourne's carbuncle began in March 1960 when Katie Juliette Underhay, a local councillor, put plans before the Borough Council to pull down Hillcote, the school on South Cliff, which had become flats. Her idea was to build in its place a tower block of high class flats, some 70m [200ft] high. After a storm of protest, the height of the building was restricted to 62m, but in 1966 the South Cliff Tower was completed, the year of her Mayoralty. A few people admire South Cliff Tower, and it is a most desirable residence in a lovely part of the town, but most folks consider it quite out of place, soaring up on the seafront, intrusive from every view, and blocking out the scene for much of South Cliff. Mrs Underhay had an apartment on the 13th floor.

There was a surge of revulsion against the building, and a determination that nothing like 'Katie's Folly' should happen again. Perhaps, rather like Peacehaven, it could be said that its presence curtailed other developments. One result was the formation of the Eastbourne Preservation Society (now the Eastbourne Society) with the aim of vetting all such planning applications. Another was that our Katie Juliette was thrown off the Council, even though it was the convention for the retiring Mayor to be re-elected unopposed. Local residents put up a non-political figure, Mrs MW Rice-Pyle, who trounced her at the polls. If politicians ever ask why there is so little interest in local government the example may be proffered that with party support Katie was put up again a few years later.

Meanwhile, an important event for Eastbourne's swimmers, anxious to ensure decent, healthy conditions for bathing, was the construction in 1965 of a new sewage outfall, with an underground pumping station near Langney Point. Another station came into use in 1979, with improvements since.

On Sunday afternoon, 20 October 1968, the tanker *Sitakund* suffered a series of explosions in the Channel, shaking the town's doors and windows, and came to rest less than a mile off Holywell, where the local Brigade controlled the fire. Part of the ship was towed away in 1969, and the rest demolished by explosive in 1972.

By the 1970s Eastbourne United FC was most famed for the managers who had started with them. Harry Haslam and Gordon Jago went on to manage First Division clubs, and Ron Greenwood was the England Soccer Manager 1977-82. The Eastbourne Rugby Football Club had joined the County Rugby Union in 1895. The team was playing at King's Drive before the 1939-45 war, and in 1969 opened a new building on the Park Avenue frontage.

The family home of Sir Kenneth Strong, chief intelligence officer to General Eisenhower, was in Ashburnham Road, and later *Kepplestone.* Cyril Scott, the composer of three symphonies, lived in Percy Grainger's old house in Pevensey Bay after 1945 and was at 53 Pashley Road from 1957 to his death in 1970. Strangely, he also wrote books with titles such as *Constipation and Commonsense.*

**Caffyns-Upperton Road new premises...**
...with the newest workshop, showroom and service facilities in town

In 1965, a century after William Caffyn opened his first shop, the company celebrated with the opening of large, prize-winning premises in Upperton Road. By now the company had a turnover of over £10m and a staff of some 1500. Caffyn's bought Clark and Lambert in the mid-1970s and Skinner's, the VW dealers, in 2002. The company also started the Eastbourne Car Show.

Some businesses were finding the going tough. Although in 1958 Bradford's had been one of the first coal merchants to sell pre-packed paper sacks, 'A boon for people in flats' and absorbed Knight's in 1971, the firm had to merge with Corralls.

Having survived the war the Beachy Head Hotel, shown here in the 1920s, burnt down on 6 April 1966. Albert Green, one of the fire-fighters explained, "It's in a vulnerable position, the wind fans the flames, and we had to ferry water up to the site." Rebuilt, it was popular for Rotary and Sunday lunches, until burnt down yet again in December 1994, whereupon Whitbread's replaced it with today's 'Brewers Fayre'.

Local government reorganisation in 1974 significantly reduced the town's importance, taking away such services as Education, Libraries, Planning, Refuse Disposal, Social Services, Transport and Fire Services - having just opened the Whitley Road Fire Station. The previous year the Magistrates Bench reverted to a petty sessional division. Eastbourne had lost its Police to the Sussex Police Authority in January 1968. New Law Courts in Old Orchard Road were opened by Lord Elwyn-Jones, Lord Chancellor, on 25 April 1975, freeing Town Hall space.

A pedestrian precinct in Terminus Road was introduced experimentally at the start of the 1970s. In Old Town the buildings adjoining Brodie's Mission Hall, probably part of the 18th century Gables school, were demolished for a car park in 1971, and the hall became the Edgmond Evangelical Church in 1993.

Over the dry, hot summer of 1976 all the surgical, obstetric and paediatric units moved from the Princess Alice and St Mary's hospitals and the Maternity Home to the new District General Hospital at Kings Drive, officially opened by Princess Alexandra the next year. The empty Maternity Home was sold in 1997 and after a few vicissitudes opened in 2000 as *Marlborough Court,* a new build.

Eastbourne is renowned for its parks and gardens, repeatedly winning Britain in Bloom Awards. Left is a floral tribute to 100 years of good work. The well-known Carpet Gardens, near the pier, contain colourful bedding plants, cacti, and fountains, surrounded by railings, but there are many other gardens and tree plantations in the town, such as the Manor House Gardens, Motcombe Gardens, Paradise, and Hampden Park.

Developments were happening to the east of the town too. Princess Diana officially opened the Sovereign Centre, Royal Parade, in June 1989, after delays and financial problems. It was revamped in 2000. The Devonshire Baths had closed at the end of 1976, with the staff transferred to the new Sovereign Pool in 1977. Not until 2003-4 was the old baths site eventually developed into more flats.

Inevitably, construction and demolition went hand in hand. St Peter's Church, Meads, (right) was suddenly knocked down in 1972 and *Redman King House* put in its place. Before the 1977-78 development of the Jesus House area in Old Town excavations by Lawrence Stevens were allowed. St Mary's Court, a residential home, now occupies that site, opposite the St Mary's Church.

The *Tivoli* closed in 1982 leaving only two cinemas in the town, the *Curzon* and the *ABC* (later *Cannon*). A new complex, however, started at the Sovereign Harbour in 1989 including restaurants, shops, and a multiplex cinema.

For more active entertainment, the Devonshire Park grass courts are world renowned, and where the top tennis stars prepare for Wimbledon. The Ball Park in Hampden Park opened 1987, and became a David Lloyd Club in 1993.

Apart from the Saffrons ground the town has other cricket associations. John Snow, the Sussex and England fast bowler, was at St Andrew's School; and Christopher Martin-Jenkins, press and radio cricket commentator, at St Bede's.

Opening the Local History Museum on 2 July 1983 was one of the centenary events commemorating Eastbourne's Incorporation. Cllr Una Goldie-Gardner was instrumental in re-establishing a museum – 40 years after the bombing. The Local History Society displays William Figg's 1816 Eastbourne map in the new museum.

In November 1983 the Mayor, Cllr Dennis Cullen, opened the Heritage Centre at 2 Carlisle Road. The building, originally the residence of the Devonshire Park Baths manager, had been leased to the Eastbourne Society who adapted it for exhibitions to the design of architect Richard Crook.

Eastbourne's Arndale Centre officially opened its doors on 7 October 1980 and transformed shopping habits in Eastbourne - apart from being detrimental to the shops in Seaside Road and Grove Road, which are only just recovering. There was a £4m refurbishment in 1997 giving natural light to the walkways, and in 2004 proposals were published for extensions to take in the station and the Enterprise Centre.

The Star Brewery in Old Town ceased brewing in 1965, but it was only after some 'eye-sore years' that the site was eventually sold to Safeway, who started building November 1983. Another bit of old Eastbourne went that autumn with the demolition of St Mary's Church School for Boys, Green Street.

Granville House was a girls' boarding school in Meads until the 1939-45 war. Afterwards the premises were bought by Eastbourne College for a prep. school, but demolished in 1984 for Gaudick Close. Dame Jean Conan Doyle, Director of the Women's Royal Air Force 1963-6, was a pupil there until her father died in 1930. Aficionados will need no reminding that Sherlock Holmes retired to a cottage on the Downs where he solved the mystery of *The Lion's Mane.* Having a daughter in Eastbourne might explain Sir Arthur's knowledge of the area.

Dorothy Stroud (1910-1997) went to yet another Meads school, Claremont, in Bolsover Road. She was the assistant curator at the Sir John Soane Museum until 1984, and her publication *Capability Brown* stimulated interest in garden history.

At last in 1984 the widening of Church Street, first mooted before the 1914-18 war, got under way. When completed Ocklynge Road, seen right before the changes, and one of the town's oldest roads, no longer had traffic access into Church Street.

The weather made news in 1987. The January temperature went down to –9C, with a fierce wind chill factor. Post was delayed, there was panic buying in the shops, garages ran out of petrol, postmen were sent to hospital with frostbitten fingers, and the newspapers ran out of headline puns and clichés - *The Big Freeze, The Big Chill, Snow Joke.* Radio stations ran *Cold Crisis Lines* or *Snowlines,* and most incredibly, but with so many burst pipes just possible, there was a more severe water shortage than in the great drought of 1976.

October 1987 felt the full blast of the 'Hurricane' which caused much damage, especially to the Paradise Drive trees, but amazingly restored by Millennium time.

Local boy, Michael Fish, the 'not a hurricane' meteorologist, opened the new Tourist Information Centre in Cornfield Road in March 1990. With tile hung walls and decorative ridge and finials it is an attractive building. A near local, Elizabeth David (1913-1992), is credited with reviving British cuisine after the war.

The Pier Company sold to Trust House in 1968/9, and Leisure Parcs paid £74m for it in 1998. The pier (right) had a narrow squeak in 1963 when a ship almost collided with it after catching fire off Beachy Head. In 1970 an arsonist fired the theatre, which was saved, but access to the camera obscura was lost until 2004. In 1982 the ballroom was converted to an Amusement Arcade and in 1987 the theatre became the Roxy discotheque and Showbar (left, fund raising for St Wilfrid's Hospice).

The gothic-styled Cavendish Place Chapel, a place of worship from 1856 to 1985, was sold to the Greek Orthodox Church in 1990 and is now dedicated to SS Panteleimon & Theodorus. Christ Church, in Seaside, still has its Willis organ, the only one on the south coast, but the congregation speaks 26 native languages.

Dinghy sailing was mainly by the Sovereign and the Eastbourne Sailing Clubs east of the pier. Now, of course, joined by surfboards and windsurfers, but the real change has been the Marina, first mooted in 1962. Parliamentary approval was not received until 1980, whereupon Tarmac Construction and Asda bought land from the Chatsworth Trustees, and Hall Aggregates, on site since 1931, closed in 1986.

The Marina project was for an outer tidal harbour, and inner marina, with residential and business development. Work commenced 1991, granite being brought from Norway for the harbour arms. On 19 February 1993 the barrier between the sea and the outer harbour at the Crumbles Marina was breached allowing the tides to flood in and out, and May saw the first boat through the lock gates. Now the 125-hectare (350 acres) Sovereign Harbour with over 1100 berths (a tiny part is shown on the back cover) stretches from Langney to Pevensey Bay.

The *Duke of Kent* lifeboat moved to the outer harbour of the Marina in 1993, and in 1994 a new lifeboat station was built near the lock gates.

To comply with the 1926/29 Downland Purchase intent of free access, in 1993 the Eastbourne Borough Council opened up additional areas of Beachy Head for the public. In 1996 more land near Bullock Down was made available.

Eastbourne, meanwhile, had a scandal brewing worthy to be put alongside Thomas Hopley, Major Teale (the Chief Constable who gave false evidence in 1918), Alderman Chatfield (involved in bribery charges in the 1930s), Caleb Diplock's will, Dr Bodkin Adams and Katie Underhay. In 1974 Graham Durnford Ford started a solicitor's office in Hastings, and opened branch offices in Polegate

1976, Eastbourne 1977, Ashford 1978, Hailsham, Bexhill, Battle, London, Rye, and finally Seaford in 1986; soon the firm had a salaried workforce of around 250. Early in 1992 evidence of financial irregularity surfaced and the firm collapsed that year causing the largest claim, of £9m, on the Law Society's Compensation Fund. Mr Ford was made bankrupt, struck off the Roll in 1993, and two years later convicted of fraud and sentenced to ten years' imprisonment.

Haughton's Corner, in Seaside Road, was the scene of another collapse in 1993. Named after a typical postcard, bucket and spade shop, it was undergoing alteration into shops and flats when the buildings fell down, because the 1870 interior walls were not of brick, but unshaped greensand nodules covered with plaster.

The Water Company lost its separate identity when it amalgamated with two other water supply undertakings on 1 March 1993. Since 1945 it had taken over Hailsham, Heathfield and Bexhill, and in 1971 constructed the Arlington Reservoir, which supplies Hampden Park, Stone Cross, and Langney. Headings at Friston, Hodcombe, and Holywell, with reservoirs at Meads and Paradise supply Meads.

Tourism remains important, but the days of bathing machines, whole families booking for a fortnight, and holidaymakers coming back year after year, have gone. The idea of emulating Lewis Carroll, who returned to the same Lushington Road landlady for 22 summers, bringing his own tin bath with him, is unthinkable. The hotels are full during special attractions, but the short break is now the rule.

After standing empty for years the Albion Hotel, Marine Parade, dating from the 1830s, was modernised in 1996 and reopened the next year as the Carlton.

A constructive approach was Sainsbury's Cross Levels Way. Built in 1993, to allow the company to have a superstore near Hampden Park, it meant cars avoided the level crossing at Hampden Park, but traffic across Kings Drive was increased.

Most of the big stores have been replaced with more specialist shops as well as 'bargain basements'. Until the 1980s Grove Road was often termed the Bond Street of Eastbourne, but with the closure of Girling's Fashions, Chocolatiers, Strange the Printer, and Jackson's Furs, one of the few old shops left is Hope & Co. Harry Clarke started the shop in Seaside Road in 1894, and it is now run by a grandson.

The season-long summer shows have lost popularity, and been replaced by touring musicals and in-house productions, combined with the Redoubt's 1812 concerts and the Bandstand's mix from Gilbert and Sullivan to rock and roll.

The Causeway Senior School opened in September 1998 responding to the housing boom to the east of the town. The intake was 140 but is projected to grow to 900. As the school is near the Shinewater Bronze Age site, an ear of wheat and a sickle were incorporated into its badge. Another new school, Haven Primary, was built at Atlantic Drive on the Sovereign Village Estate.

Brighton University, formerly Brighton Polytechnic, includes colleges in Eastbourne, mainly at Meads. The Podiatry School is in the old Leaf Hospital.

Our Lady of Ransom Church, the Congress Theatre, and the Grand Parade Bandstand were listed. Sadly, the bandstand was showing its age and needed work to prevent further deterioration. One long-standing tradition, continued into the 21st century, has the Boxing Day dancers turning out in force for Malcolm Cornford leading the Sounds Easy band. Whether the Military Bands, an immense draw during the summer, will continue is a matter of some conjecture.

From 1997 to 1999 new groynes were constructed and extra shingle brought in for the beach. The 500m section between the pier and the West Beach bathing cabins is patrolled by lifeguards during the season.

The Eastbourne lifeboats (the *Royal Thames* and an inflatable) saved 17 lives and had 112 calls in 1998. The coastguards were presented with the 2001 Rescue Shield Award Trophy in recognition of their Beachy Head rescues and recoveries.

The Council and commerce aim to appeal to all interests with entertainment such as Airbourne (right) and to keep the town attractive to all by many 'Change Your View' ventures, which include the resiting of the 1865 Seaside Drinking Fountain to Seahouses Square (left) at a ceremony in December 2000.

The attractive Eastbourne seafront is unique in that there are no shops along its three miles, thanks to restrictive covenants enforced by the Dukes of Devonshire, however, there are suggestions that restaurants may be allowed. Shortly before his death in 2004 Eastbourne Borough Council fittingly made Andrew, 11th Duke of Devonshire, an honorary Freeman of the Borough in recognition of his role as a major landowner, for his involvement in the town's many clubs and institutions, and because he was a good friend of Eastbourne.

Royal interest has also continued since 1780. Recently Prince Charles visited to open Age Concern's Venton Centre in Junction Road; and the Duke of York came for the new Jubilee Eye Unit at the District General Hospital in 2004.

The award of £5m from central funds will mean the town can build a much needed Conference, Exhibition and Cultural Centre on Devonshire Park, which will house the Towner Art Gallery, cafés and other community amenities.

So, cosseted by Beachy Head, Eastbourne, now 95 000 strong, keeps its suntrap image, holds its reputation for safe sea bathing, and maintains its welcoming tradition while accommodating the more fickle demands of today's holidaymakers.

# INDEX

(Page number in **Bold** if illustrated)